Ghost Towns of Washington and Oregon

Ghost Towns of Washington and Oregon

By

Donald C. Miller

PRUETT **P** PUBLISHING COMPANY
Boulder, Colorado

First Edition
1 2 3 4 5 6 7 8 9

Library of Congress Cataloging in Publication Data

Miller, Don C
    Ghost towns of Washington and Oregon.

    Includes bibliographical references and index.
    1.   Cities and towns, Ruined, extinct, etc. — Washington
(State). 2.   Cities and towns, Ruins, extinct, etc. — Oregon.
3.   Washington (State) — History, local. 4.   Oregon — History,
Local. I. Title.
F891.M54   979.7   77-24428
ISBN 0-87108-500-3

Printed in the United States of America

All photographs by Don Miller unless otherwise acknowledged.
Editing was done by Robert C. McGiffert.

Contents

Foreword

Washington has never been classified as a major mining state,[1] yet it boasts two gold-producing areas that rank in the top ten in the nation.[2]

In 1853 Captain George McClennand and his railroad-route exploring party found gold in the Yakima River valley. Prospecting was carried out in the Colville district as early as 1855, the year placers were first worked along the Pend Oreille and Columbia rivers. During the 1858–60 period, mining excitement centered on the Blewett Pass area.

As the placers petered out, attention turned to lode mining. Soon the Republic, Oreville-Nighthawk, Monte Cristo, Mount Baker, Slate Creek, and Wenatchee districts resounded with the cacophony of mining activity. Gold production was estimated at about 3 million ounces.[3]

Oregon's first known placers were worked at Rich Gulch in Jackson County and Josephine Creek in Josephine County. Discoveries of placer gold at Griffin Gulch in Baker County and at John Day and Canyon Creek in Grant County in the 1860s caused the gold-hungry to stampede to the area. During this period, gold-bearing quartz veins were also worked. When the (gold) dust settled, production in Oregon came to about 5,796,680 ounces.[4]

The 1870 Oregon census lists a total of 3,965 miners, of whom 2,428 were Chinese.[5]

The gold-seekers left indelible marks on the land and its people. They led fluid lives, scurrying from place to place. The Oregon men particularly were so crazed by gold fever that when they heard news of the California gold strike, perhaps two-thirds of them started for California.[6] The territorial legislature had to be suspended for lack of a quorum.[7]

Bullwhackers, saloon keepers, prospectors, undertakers, prostitutes, gamblers, and blacksmiths coursed through the dusty streets of the mining camps. Later came the "respectable" women, lawmen, and preachers, but not always before Judge Lynch had presided at trials in which the victim "died of a fall when the platform on which he stood fell away." As men found and fought for gold, they left a permanent legacy.

In the Washington and Oregon ghost towns the visitor can scuff through the ashes of old dreams. And in the remnants of these mining camps is borne out the idea that often natural things, when they die, die so much more gracefully than that made by man. But in capturing something of what *is still* there, it is possible to imagine what *was* there.

Enough remains of many of these "playthings of the wind" to sense the good and the bad, the strong and the weak, the admirable and the contemptible in their inhabitants.

Some mining camps remain robust. But many are fragile as roses pressed for years between pages in a dusty, musty book. These dead or dying ghosts are the subject of this nostalgic look at the mouldering memorabilia of a colorful, kaleidoscopic past.

Washington

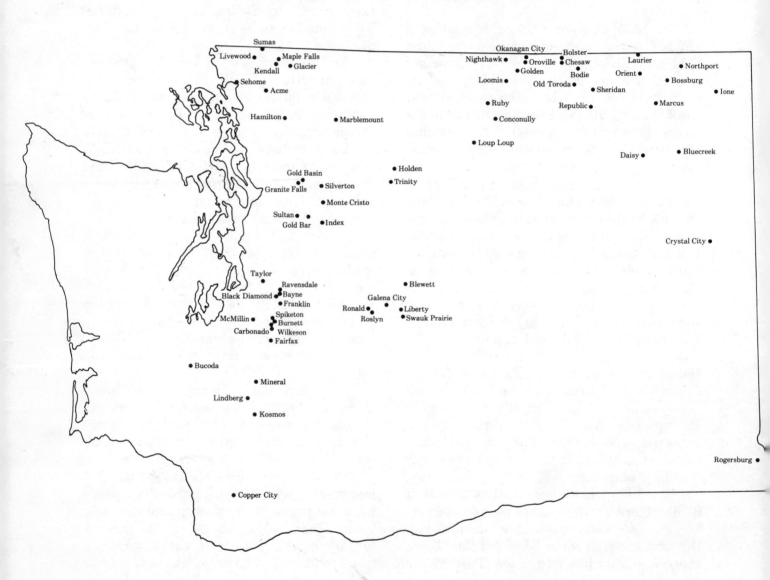

Sumas
Livewood
Maple Falls
Kendall • Glacier
Sehome
Acme
Hamilton • Marblemount

Okanagan City
Bolster
Nighthawk • Oroville • Chesaw
Laurier
Northport
Golden • Bodie
Orient
Bossburg
Loomis
Old Toroda
Sheridan
Ione
Ruby
Republic
Marcus
Conconully

Loup Loup

Daisy
Bluecreek

Holden
Gold Basin
Trinity
Granite Falls • Silverton

Monte Cristo
Sultan
Gold Bar • Index

Crystal City

Taylor
Ravensdale
Blewett
Black Diamond • Bayne
Galena City
Franklin
Ronald
Liberty
McMillin
Spiketon
Roslyn • Swauk Prairie
Carbonado • Burnett
Wilkeson
Fairfax

Bucoda

Mineral
Lindberg
Kosmos

Rogersburg

Copper City

Acme lives on, east of Bellingham.

Early prospecting took place above the town on the South Fork of the Nooksack River. Records indicate that a prospecting party arrived there as early as August 1860.[8]

Bayne was a coal-mining town about fifteen miles east of Auburn.

The beginnings of the settlement are vague, but apparently the town began in the 1880s, and by 1908 rich coal seams had been found and were being worked in the area. The prime, if not sole, operator was the Green River Coal Company.[9]

Black Diamond still exists east of Auburn.

Coal development began in the area in 1890, and by 1895 the Black Diamond mines attained, and for several years maintained, the role of King County's biggest producer.[10] But Black Diamond mines were killers. In the decade from 1900 to 1910, three major mine explosions claimed thirty-four lives (eleven in 1902, seven in 1907, and sixteen in 1910).[11]

The settlement was named for the California-based Black Diamond Coal Company.

In 1941 the town was described as having "a shabby, ancient depot and a few uniform ramshackle frame houses, which perch on the brow of a hill, and at certain times of the year cows may be seen grazing in the streets."[12]

Bluecreek survives northwest of Chewalah, on Highway 395. It was once a mining and shipping center for copper and dolomite mines in the area.

Addy is immediately north of Bluecreek. It also was a supply and transportation center for area mines.

Gold was discovered in the **Blewett** area probably in 1855-56[13] by a Captain Ingalls and an Indian named Colowah. Ingalls later returned to the area but lost both the gold strike site and his life.

In 1860 a rush to the Peshastin Creek[14] area helped to lead to the founding of Blewett. Initially, only placers were worked, with varying degrees of success. One black man took out more than $1,000 in a single mining season from the bars at the mouth of Negro Creek.

Not until 1874[15] or 1879[16] was the first lode mining undertaken.

Several claims were bought and consolidated by James Lockwood, his son E.W., and H. M. Cooper, who erected a water-powered, six-stamp mill. The cleanup from the first nine day's run was reported at $2,100.[17] The men also built a 1,000-ton capacity arrastre. The partners mined for eight years, then sold their holdings. Shortly thereafter the mines were closed. The properties were resold in 1891, a ten-stamp mill was erected, and a tramway was built, but by the next year the properties were again deserted. Later, a twenty-stamp mill was erected, but by 1894 the company began leasing parts of the mines to small miners' associations.

The town of Blewett and area mines were prospering near the turn of the century. It has been estimated that 10,000 gold bricks were shipped from the town every week.[18] Since it is not known over what period of time gold shipments were made, and since the United States Geological Survey estimates total gold production from the Blewett (Penhastin) district between 1870 and 1959 at about 850,900 ounces,[19] the 10,000 figure is suspect.

After 1910 only limited mining activity occurred in the area, and Blewett became a "wide spot in the road"—actually a spot on both sides of a road: Highway 97, which cuts through the middle of town. On one side of the highway are two of the original buildings.

Two buildings sandwiched together at Acme.

A "moody" cabin at Acme.

4

The old cream station at Addy.

The "welcome to Black Diamond" sign and display.

Bluecreek

Bodie is located north of Wauconda and south of Chesaw in northeastern Washington.

The mining town was laid out along Toroda Creek in about the year 1900.

Bodie was a company town of The Perkins Milling Company.

At one time the settlement consisted of a store, post office, cookhouse, bunkhouse, and hotel. A stamp mill processed ores from the Golden Reward and Elk (Golconda) mines until the late 1930s. The stamp mill stood until 1962,[20] when fire consumed it.

Bolster was immediately north of Chesaw.

The town was probably christened by J. S. McBride in 1899. McBride had recently bought the Commonwealth placer claim and decided that a town needed to be established nearby.

The gleam in McBride's eye grew to reality in the form of a post office, a couple of stores, three saloons, thirty houses, and a newspaper—The *Bolster Drill.*

But mining towns cannot be sustained on dreams, and as mining ventures failed, so did the town. Perhaps illustrative of half-filled dreams was the never-completed Bolster hotel.

The post office was closed in 1909. School opened for only one year—in 1910. The story is told that by the beginning of World War I only seven bachelor prospectors inhabited the ephemeral town, but finally they all left—or died.[21]

Bossburg was first called Young America, then Millington, and finally Bossburg.

The original name was bestowed in honor of the Young America galena ore mine, established about 1888. In 1893 the town was platted and called Millington. The third—and final—name change was made about 1896, when the settlement was called Bossburg in honor of C. S. Boss, one of the town's leading citizens.

The sign on this cabin at Bodie reminds visitors that it's private property and that "survivors will be prosecuted."

A sometimes-lived-in cabin at Bodie.

The school at Bodie.

Extant **Bucoda** is northeast of Centralia, beside the Shookumchuck River.

The village began as a lumbering community in 1854 after Aaron Webster settled there. The Indians called the town that grew up around the sawmill "seatco"; and Seatco the community was called for about one third of a century.

When coal was discovered across the Shookumchuck, John David, John Buckley, and Samuel Coulter brought in capital for mine development. (The town was named from the first syllables of the three names—BUckley, COulter and DAvid.) Somehow the town became the site of the territory's first penitentiary.

Convict labor was used at the coal mines and at nearby logging camps. A furor arose over the practice, and for these and other reasons the prison was removed to Walla Walla in 1887.

Burnett was founded south of Buckley around 1881. About 1884 it was named for pioneer mine operator Charles H. Burnett.

By 1898 about sixty houses were located along South Prairie Creek in Lower (older) Burnett. In addition to houses, Burnett had the usual outhouses, but they extended over the creek. During spring high water, many were regularly washed away.

On December 7, 1904, a mine explosion in the South Prairie Coal Company's No. 5 mine killed seventeen. An explosion in the Burnett mine in 1918 killed twelve.

By 1917 Burnett's population neared 500, about 300 of whom were employed by the company. There were at least three halls in town: the Union, Finn, and Forester's halls. In about 1920 the company built a two-story hotel, a store, a dance hall, and a garage with a billiard hall in back.

The company payroll was brought to town in a Model T truck which resembled a dogcatcher's wagon.[22]

Mining became unprofitable in 1927, and the next year the houses and land were offered for sale. Some buildings were moved, but many were torn down, including the hotel, dance hall, and company store. The schoolhouse burned to the ground.

Tattered remains of early coal mining days remain in this somnolent village.

A gate leads to some cooking utensils . . . only, at Burnett.

A strange structure at Carbonado.

Carbonado is immediately south of Wilkeson on Highway 5 leading south to Mount Rainier National Park.

This company town almost died when the Pacific Coast Coal Company abandoned operations there in the late 1920s.

Forty-eight miners died in two coal mine explosions at Carbonado. The Carbon Hill No. 7 mine explosion on December 9, 1899, killed thirty-one persons. The April 12, 1930, explosion took seventeen lives. A United States Bureau of Mines report described that scene:

An explosion in 2d level workings in Douty No. 8 bed at about 5:30 p.m. killed all of the 17 men in the section. The Bureau of Mines rescue truck was called from Seattle, and rescue crews recovered the bodies by 1 a.m. the next morning. Ventilation was easily restored, and apparatus men made explorations ahead.

The explosion originated at the face of No. 5 chute, when two holes were fired in the presence of gas. The holes were loaded with permissible explosive and fired electrically; however, they were overloaded, and either one might have been almost an open shot, as the other could have broken out all the burden. The chute was dry and the air very dusty. The face was ventilated by compressed air only. The explosion was propagated and probably initiated by a mixture of gas and dust. No watering was done and no rock dust used. Some of the workings were wet, and this limited the explosion.[23]

The town had paved streets and a sophisticated sewage system. It fostered soccer and baseball teams, fraternal organizations, and societies.

Company houses rented for an average of fourteen dollars a month.[24]

The old Carbonado mine still squats near the town, flooded because the coal company long ago removed pumps used to clear the mine of water.

Cedar Canyon (Cedarville) grew up north of Davenport and southeast of Fruitland. It was once said that the town "transacts considerable business with the Lincoln County mining industries in the way of mining and other supplies."[25]

The first gold discovery in the area was supposedly made by a bankrupt farmer who, although ignorant of mining, managed to strike it rich.

Very little is known of this now vanished settlement, which, to begin with, probably had no more than thirty-three town lots.[26]

Chesaw was established east of Oroville. It was named for "Chee-Saw," an early Chinese settler who lived there with his Indian wife. They set up a sort of hostelry referred to by some as a "bungaloo."[27]

When this Indian land was thrown open to whites in 1896,[28] Chesaw began to grow. By the turn of the century there were perhaps 200 people in town, several substantial structures including two three-story hotels, and a newspaper (The *Meyers Creek News*). In 1906 one hotel burned to the ground, and in 1908 three more of the town's larger structures burned.

One by one, businesses closed, and the town began to die. Josh Clary's Greenwood Saloon was sold and converted into a church. A steeple that was tacked onto the roof extended just slightly over the saloon's false front.

Fires racked the town in 1950 and again in 1959, leading further to the town's demise.

The Chesaw Store. Several signs in town advise, "No Drinking in Public."

Chesaw, 1899 — *From William C. Brown papers,
Washington State University Library.*

Structures near Chesaw.

Tower at Chesaw.

Conconully. Photo by Frank S. Matsura in the early spring of 1906. This photo is commonly called the Deserted Village for not a living thing is anywhere in sight—*From William C. Brown papers, Washington State University Library.*

Conconully probably began in 1886[29] when prospectors rushed to the Salmon Creek district. (Until 1888 the settlement was known as Salmon City, named for Salmon Creek, which flowed through the town.) Since they had arrived in the spring, the prospectors first lived in tents, which were replaced by cabins in the autumn.

In 1888 Conconully became the county seat.[30] Four years later a roaring fire nearly destroyed it, and in 1893, after Congress killed the Silver Act, the beleaguered town was crippled even more.[31] In May 1894 a flood thundered down on the settlement, washing away forty-two buildings. Only one death was reported, however.

Leading mines were the Tough Nut and the Lone Star. In about 1887 former Lieutenant Governor Charles Laughton organized a mining company and erected a concentrator in the canyon between the two mines. One observer wrote, "But much of the mineral escaped with the tailings, so that the latter were richer than the concentrates, less than half the value being saved."[32] After a two-week run, the concentrator was closed, never to run again.

But the little village still lives, with old false-fronted buildings acting as reminders of palmier days. Conconully is now a resort/summer home site.

Copper City was a short-lived copper and gold boom town. It was brought to its knees by the Yalcolt Burn of 1902, a forest fire that stopped mining activity.

A man named Sam Pumpelly took samples of rich ore from a mine and placed them in the worthless Copper City mine. But his salting did not pan out, and no gullible buyers were lured by his scheme. Pumpelly died shortly afterward, and since then the evanescent settlement has slowly mouldered along Copper Creek, near Amboy in Clark County.

Although there are mostly new summer cabins at Conconully, a few older structures dot the landscape.

A log doghouse at Conconully.

The history of **Crystal City** is not exactly crystal clear.

Apparently the town site on the banks of the Spokane River, just above the site of old Fort Spokane, was laid out December 23, 1903, by B. W. Wolverton.

The town appears to have been a successor to Grayville, born in May 1899. Grayville, it seems, was earlier called Miles, a settlement established in the early 1880s.

Crystal City was located near the Crystal mine, as were its predecessors. Grayville apparently began to lose itself as an entity after July 10, 1899, when a fire swept through town. The record simply states, "Since that event [the fire] Grayville appears to have languished until it was supplanted by the new town of Crystal City."[33]

The hillside settlement of **Daisy**, located near Inchelium (or Gifford), near Highway 25 in northeastern Washington, was abandoned when the Grand Coulee dam flooded the locality.

Two silver-lead mines—the Tempest and the Daisy—were worked in the area for several years.

In the same region is the Silver Queen mine, not to be confused with the Old Queen mine near Fruitland.

Fairfax was once a flourishing coal mining and lumbering town in the Carbon River canyon.

Although mining commenced there in 1896, records of The Western American Company indicate that no production occurred until 1900.

Apparently white, black, and then Chinese miners toiled successively in the Fairfax-area mines.

The company built twenty-five coke ovens in 1900 and thirty-five more in 1907, giving a 2,500-ton monthly capacity. The Tacoma Smelting Company bought the properties in 1907 and worked them until 1911. During that year a new mine was opened, with at least part of the operation being owned by the Fairfax Mine, Inc. Later the properties were purchased by the Wilkerson Coal and Coke Company. But soon mining operations ceased and Fairfax withered.

Deserted structures built by the Eaton-ville Lumber Company squat across the Carbon River from the inhabited part of town. A depot, a service station, a shingle mill, mine bunkers, a schoolhouse, and a few other relics of better days dot the landscape.

Franklin was a coal-spawned company town between Enumclaw and Black Diamond. The Oregon Improvement Company employed about 450 miners, while the town itself consisted of about 100 persons in 1888.

Coal bunkers, a company store, a hotel, a boarding house, a blacksmith shop, a meat market, two saloons, and a schoolhouse (which served as a church on Sunday) composed the town of Franklin.

All that remains is a cemetery where most of the thirty-seven miners killed in a mine disaster August 24, 1894, are buried.

Galena was located in the Index area, as were the mining camps of Mineral City and Monte Cristo. All were in the Monte Cristo mining district.

Mining occurred in the Galena vicinity in the 1880s, but the town was not platted until December 1891.

Little is known of the camp, and no production statistics for mines in the Monte Cristo district have been issued since 1918. The ghost towns of the district are veiled in obscurity.

Gold Bar, east of Sultan, began as a prospectors' camp in 1889 after gold was found along a river bar.

An unusual target in a back yard in Gold Bar.

The "basement entrance" to Ann's Tavern in Gold Bar.

Later, Gold Bar became a Great Northern Railroad construction camp where anti-Chinese sentiment first festered, then erupted. To save the Chinese, a railroad construction engineer shipped them out of camp in hastily built coffins.

Gold Basin, in the Granite Falls region, was the center of a mining area, but little exists on record about this camp near the Verlot forest ranger station.

Golden, a vanished mining town near Wanacut Lake, once had a population of perhaps 500.

Apparently the town had stage connections, for in 1897 prospectors bound for Golden were instructed to go by stage the seventy miles from Brewster, or the twenty-eight miles from Johnson Creek.[34]

Gold Hill City (Shuksan) came into being on the south end of Palmer Mountain because of the 1892[35] gold quartz discoveries of John Reed and "Irish" Dan McCauley. The settlement was situated above Loomis. The mines were later developed by the Gold Hill Mining Company.

Road washouts between Gold Hill and Loomis caused problems, but because of the limited quantity and quality of the gold, it was decided that mining returns did not justify building a better road, and the entire Gold Hill project was abandoned about 1910.

Other settlements were located in the same general area of the Mount Baker mining district. So many prospectors swarmed the camps that by February 1898 Whatcom County's largest voting precinct—the Swamp Creek district—was established along what was known as The State Trail. The communities that grew up along the trail included **Trail City**, located one mile above Gold Hill City at the mouth of Swamp Creek; **Wilson's City** (or Wilson's Townsite), two miles above Trail City at the mouth of Ruth Creek; **Gold City**, two miles above Wilson's City; and **Union City**, near Twin Lakes, one mile above Gold City.[36]

But when all the dust had settled and the mining excitement passed, only two good producing mines emerged from the 3,000 mining claims in Whatcom County's Mount Baker district—the Post-Lambert group, or Lone Jack mine; and the Boundary Red Mountain mine.

Granite Falls, between the South Fork of the Stillaguamish River and the Pilchuck River, was born as a mining camp but evolved into an agricultural-lumbering settlement.

There were copper, gold, and silver prospects aplenty in the area, and the future looked good for major mining developments. A small stamp mill was erected and noisily dropped its heavy stamps for a while, but the gods of gold were not to smile favorably on Granite Falls.

The population has remained at about 600 during the past half century, so the settlement does not seem likely to join the roster of ghosts.

17

cased by high water of the Skagit Rive
in the year
of 1896

Front street Hamilton Wash.
Photo By L Heath Nov. 3, 1898.

Damage on Front Street at Hamilton in 1896 from the flood-swollen Skagit River — *Photog-* *raphy Collection, Suzzallo Library, University of Washington.*

Hamilton, on Highway 16 west of Concrete, lies in what is termed the Skagit copper belt.

The principal discoveries were made on Iron Mountain, on the south bank of the Skagit River, opposite the townsite.

Because of the area's low elevation and mild temperatures, mining could be carried on almost year around.

Hamilton was the eastern terminus of the Seattle & Northern Railroad, which put the town within sixty-eight miles of the Everett smelter and 135 miles from the Tacoma smelter. Another plus factor in the

community's development is the fact that the Skagit River was navigable to the townsite for most steamers.

The town still endures.

It is not clear when **Holden** (near Lake Chelan) was established. It was a company town owned by the Howe Sound Company. About 600 persons were employed by the company, which extracted about 200 million pounds of copper, 40 million pounds of zinc, and unrecorded quantities of gold and silver from the area.

When the big copper producer—the D-Day mine—was closed June 28, 1957, the

The Cascade Market and Service Station at Hamilton.

town expired. The mine closing meant the abandonment of 100 private houses, six bunkhouses, a hospital, a school, and fourteen company homes. It is reported that some of the private houses sold two for one dollar, and many found new uses as chicken coops.

The *Tacoma News Tribune* mused in its June 9, 1957, issue that "Once the mine is sealed and water fills its shaft, there is little likelihood the operation—and Holden—ever will come back to life." Very prophetic.

Ione's mining history evolved from neither gold nor silver, but rather from cement.

In either 1904[37] or 1906[38] a Portland cement plant was built a short distance north of Ione. This was perhaps the first attempt to make cement in Washington, but the plant was a failure. In 1934 the abandoned cement plant was destroyed by fire.

The town survives, however, and with a population of about 650 is the second largest town in Pend Oreille County.

Tweety's place in Ione.

The deserted Ione school.

The Heidi & (?) Don Tavern and Cafe in Metaline Falls.

The Metaline laundromat, which shares part of a building occupied by Jack's and Phyl's Drive-In.

North of Ione, on Highway 6, are **Metaline** and **Metaline Falls**. Metaline was given life by the Pend Oreille Mine and Metal Company's plant, while the Mammoth and Morning mines lured people to Metaline Falls in 1910. Silver, lead, cement materials, fire clay, and lime are found in the region.

Keller was founded in 1898 and named for J. C. Keller, a storekeeper who originally set up a local business in a tent.

The town was started in 1898 when the southern half of the Colville Indian reservation was opened to mining (the northern half had been opened two years earlier).

The townsite is now under about eighty feet of water from the Grand Coulee dam.

Index was in an area rich in minerals—including gold, copper, silver, antimony, molybdenum, and several arsenates.

It was named for the nearby mountain whose granite "finger" points skyward.

Amos D. Gunn, for whom nearby Gunn Peak is named, is credited with fathering Index, probably in 1889. He built a hotel to accommodate the prospectors and surveyors who came to the area. The demand for his hotel became so great that in 1891 he had to build an addition. In 1890 Gunn opened a saloon. The following year he became postmaster. He platted the town in 1893, naming it for Mount Index. Later, a second addition was built to his hotel. A hospital of sorts was established in a tent a couple of miles west of town, and a school was started in 1893 by Lena, a member of the Gunn family.

A fire hit Index on the night of July 22, 1893, burning the entire town, excluding the railroad depot and station house. As one observer put it, Mr. "Gunn rebuilt the store and hotel at once, but with the panic days at hand, the railroad built, and the mine excitement dying down, the town made but little progress during the next few years."[39]

In the 1897–99 period, mining activities again increased, but during 1899 Amos Gunn's wife, Persis, died. Wrote one historian, "It was this bereavement as well as his good business judgment which led Mr. Gunn to sell nearly all of his holdings at Index during the height of the boom, in 1899, and to live the remainder of his life in comparative retirement."[40]

Gunn may have been a prophet, for in November 1902 another fire struck the settlement, destroying the Sunset lodging house, run by Harry Hoback. Four other structures were destroyed. James Kelly was burned to death.

Over the next few years Index "enjoyed a slow but steady growth, suffering no serious reverses, and enjoying no periods of overdone prosperity."[41]

Although some of the original Index remains, "There are lots of open spaces now from which one can gaze up at the encircling [mountain] peaks."[42]

Mercury fathered and sustained **Kosmos**, near the confluence of Rainey Creek and the Cowlitz River.

About four miles from Kosmos, near a branch of Highway 5 and the Morton cinnabar mine, another town grew up, but it apparently was not named.

Kosmos has vanished, removed for Davisson Lake, created in 1969 by Tacoma City Light.

Two mining-related settlements still exist below the Canadian border on Highway 395—**Laurier** and **Orient**.

Laurier, now a port of entry, was a stopping place for wagon and pack trains in the earlier days of mining excitement.

Orient was founded as a mining camp in 1902 and was first called Morgan. It was renamed for a nearby mine.

A number of mines are still located in the area.

Property of the Talisman Mining and Leasing Company near Laurier.

Mining operations near Liberty.

The placer mining camp of **Liberty** was located on Swauk Creek. Several streams north and south of the settlement contained much gold, and Williams, Boulder, Baker, First, and Swauk creeks were almost totally staked out by prospectors. The rush started after a deaf-mute, Bent Goodwin, went to Swauk Creek for water in 1868 and made the discovery.[43] He reportedly found a nugget worth ten to twelve dollars.[44] Nuggets were so plentiful during the initial rush that the finer gold was ignored. One nugget valued at $565 was found.[45] Some say that a single pan yielded $1,365 in gold.[46]

The record is unclear, but it appears that the community established at the point of first discovery may have been called Meaghersville, and that as mining activity moved upstream, so did the settlement that was later (in 1900)[47] dubbed Liberty. The town may have reached a peak population of 3,000.[48]

When news of big strikes in the Yukon reached Liberty, the town became a ghost.

In 1925 dredging operations brought new life to the settlement. During the Depression some mining activities occurred, but they were of a sporadic nature.

Small-scale gold mining was resumed in 1965, and still continues near this sleepy little community.

C. B. Kellson's Hope Prospect mine, June 1914 at Liberty — *Photography Collection, Suzzallo Library, University of Washington.*

Lindberg, a logging and mining settlement, was on old Highway 5, near Morton.

Some mill ruins and the remains of brick cottages, company shacks, and a store mark the spot where the town grew up, then died.

Livewood was established in 1885 at the mouth of Skookum Creek in the Nooksack mining district.

W. D. Jenkins wrote from Livewood on August 31, 1885, that the district was full of prospectors, but that few "had got down to business."[49] Little wonder that not too many gold seekers were hard at work, for the richest pan yielded only twelve cents.[50]

Perhaps the words of H. P. O'Brien, a mining expert, should have been heeded. He reported from the Nooksack district that gold prospectors were good, but that agricultural prospects were better.[51]

Loop Loop was established about 1890 in the Conconully area.

Its life and death story differs little from that of thousands of other mining camps. Decreasing prices for precious metals and increasing costs of mining and living led to its demise.

When the camp was abandoned, all that remained was one building and a brickyard. Today all traces of this mining camp have disappeared.

Marblemount was once a supply base for prospectors.

The settlement obtained its name from the marble quarry west of town. Copper was known to be in the Skagit foothills beyond Marblemount. Reportedly, quartz deposits containing copper and gold, and some signs of nickel, were found along Dispasi Creek, about five miles above Marblemount.[54]

Loomis, southwest of Oroville, began as a ranching-farming center in the early 1870s. But catastrophies like the bitter winter of 1879–80, which wiped out the 3,000-head cattle herd of Phelps Wadleigh and Company, turned many in the area to gold, silver, and copper mining. Most mineral discoveries in the area date to 1880. The Loomis post office was established in 1888.

A five-stamp mill was erected at the site and ran for five months in 1892. It produced $113,000[52] in gold, but because its gold recovery capabilities were limited, the operation was closed. In 1895 the machinery was repaired and used again, but at small profit.

Musical miners formed a band that performed in Loomis and surrounding camps, charging $100 per performance.[53]

In 1927 the last operating mine in the area closed, and the small, still-surviving community joined the roster of Washington ghost towns.

In Washington's history there stands a "New" **Marcus** and an "Old" **Marcus**. The former still exists; the latter, former hub of fourteen gold mining camps,[55] is now inundated by Columbia River waters which were backed up by the Grand Coulee Dam.

The settlement was the oldest town in Stevens County and was the site of sluicing operations during the 1860s and 1870s, mostly by Chinese.

The "fire station" at Marcus.

McMillin still survives southeast of Tacoma. Although the community is now geared to agriculture, it was spawned by lime mining, which began in the vicinity in 1877. The townsite was platted May 17, 1889.

The town appears to have been named by officials of the Roche Harbor Lime Company in honor of company president John S. McMillin.[56]

Mineral City is another "mystery" camp in the shadowy history of the enigmatic Monte Cristo mining district.

A tale is told of a packer on his way to either Mineral City or nearby Galena. It seems that his horse shied and bucked loose some dynamite, scattering the sticks over the ground. Mules in the pack train hungrily chomped up the explosives. The frightened packer managed to get his string of animals together and headed in the right direction, but he kept a discreet distance behind the train. Rumor has it that he didn't hit a single mule for the entire summer, for fear he might set off the dynamite sticks.

A surface vein of red realgar (from which arsenic is extracted) was mined near Mineral City for twenty-two years. But modern technology made conventional arsenic mining uneconomical, and the resourceful residents of Mineral turned to logging for a livelihood.

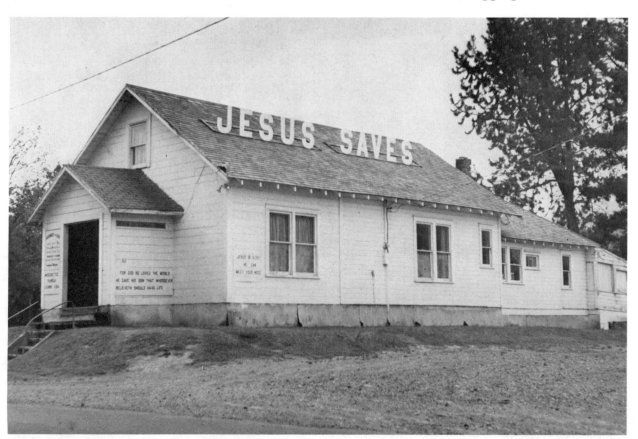

The Assembly of God church at Mineral.

Monte Cristo was about forty miles east of Everett in the Monte Cristo mining district, on the west slope of the Cascade Range.

The first strikes in the area were made by F. W. Peabody and Joe Pearsoll in 1889.

The camp was named in 1890, the year in which a trail was hacked out between Monte Cristo and its sister mining camp, Mineral City.

Rockefeller family interests bought area mines, consolidated operations, invested in a 200-ton concentrator, and in 1893 built a railroad into the town at an estimated cost of $2 million.[57]

By the summer of 1894, Monte Cristo boasted all the accoutrements of a typical boom town, including a partially completed log jail. The jail never was finished; it was torn down and thrown into Silver Creek. The jail-destroyers left a note consisting of a skull and crossbones and a vigilante signature—"4-11-44."[58]

Wolle[59] estimates that mines near Monte Cristo produced over $6 million worth of precious metals. The United States Geological Survey puts the figure for the entire Monte Cristo mining district at about $3.5 million.[60]

The privately owned Monte Cristo site is fairly well preserved, its most imposing structure being the lodge, the "rehabilitated" cook house of the Boston-American Mining Company.

James Kyes store at Monte Cristo, 1902 — *Photography Collection, Suzzallo Library, University of Washington.*

The cook house of the Del Campo Company mine
at Monte Cristo — *Photography Collection,
Suzzallo Library, University of Washington.*

The Del Campo mine at Monte Cristo — *Photography Collection, Suzzallo Library, University of
Washington.*

The lodge at Monte Cristo.

Newcastle was a coal camp not far from Seattle.

The town was along the Seattle-Walla Walla Railroad, built in the 1870s by investors from Seattle. It is not known when the camp was abandoned.

A coal strip-mining operation was located nearby, along Coal Creek Gulch.

Nighthawk (near Palmer Lake) was a mining camp named for the nighthawks, or bullbats, which frequented the Similkameen River.

The town was across the river from the mines. During Nighthawk's early years, a footbridge spanned the river, but later William Berry put a ferry into operation. The enterprising Berry started a saloon in partnership with his brother, Joe. As one commentator wrote: "It was a success in summer when the dry and dusty wind blew, a success in winter when at forty below a man needed warming."[61]

Today a tiny general store is the only operating business in Nighthawk.

Northport (established in 1892) came to life as a meteoric mining town when the $250,000 LeRoy Smelter (later to become the Day Smelter) was "blown in" during 1898[62] by the Union Smelting and Refining Company.[63]

Five hundred men were employed at the smelter, which was supplied mostly by ores from the LeRoy and Silver Star mines near Rossland, British Columbia. Smaller quantities of ore came from nearby Red Top Mountain and Cedar, Deep, and Onion creeks, on the United States side of the boundary.[64]

Northport had at least an average number of "gloomers," or "highgraders"—people who stole as much of the richest ores as they could from mines, assay offices, smelters, wherever. In 1900 one highgrader "did himself in." He was a smelter employee who had highgraded enough ore to fill a big trunk. The man bought a train ticket[65] to Spokane, where he thought he could sell the ore. He had the trunk ticketed as baggage, but, as one story goes, "When he sought to retrieve the trunk by presenting his claim check, he found the railroad company asking a large payment for overweight. This so enraged him that he refused to pay. The railroad company opened the trunk, discovered the ore, and notified the police. The man served a year in jail."[66]

Abandoned railroad tracks near Nighthawk.

Riverside Street, Northport, Washington —
Courtesy Eastern Washington State Historical Society.

A grocery store at Northport.

Okanogan waterfront, 1908 — *From William C. Brown papers, Washington State University Library.*

Okanogan City was established near Oroville. It was named for Hiram F. "Okanogan" Smith, who came to the area in 1858—the year before gold was discovered there.

Members of the Boundary Commission, trying to establish the United States–Canadian boundary lines, were the first to find gold along the banks of the Similkameen River.

The town that grew up in the center of the mining activity exploded to a population of perhaps 3,000 within one week of its founding.[67] But news of other strikes siphoned off almost the entire population of Okanogan City.

Although some miners and prospectors returned briefly to the settlement, before long it was lifeless, and has now vanished.

Old Toroda is located northeast of Wauconda.

Little is known of this vacant mining camp, which still contains the gaunt structures of a post office, an assayer's office, the Schmeling general store, a blacksmith shop, and several cabins.

The camp sprang into being in the late 1890s and probably reached its peak population about 1898.

Toroda, Washington — *Courtesy Eastern Washington State Historical Society.*

The blacksmith shop at Old Toroda. To the right
is the Schmeling General Store.

The assay office at Old Toroda.

Orient is situated along U.S. Highway 395, one dozen miles south of the Canadian border.

Gold discoveries on nearby First Thought Mountain were responsible for the establishment of the settlement, first platted in 1900 by Alec Ireland.

George Temple started a dray line, hauling machinery for area hardrock mines such as the Gold Stake, Easter Sunday, Little Gem, First Thought, and Orient (after which the town was named).

Railroad construction gangs joined the miners in helping the town to boom.

But when the railroad was completed and the crews and camp followers left, recovery costs began to exceed ore payments, and one by one the mines closed.

Today Orient residents admit they've seen better days.

City Hall (?) at Orient.

The Orient office of the Big Nine Mine and Mineral, Inc. firm.

Oroville still exists south of the Canadian border along Highway 97.

The town was first called "Ore," but later the United States Post Office changed the name in order to avoid confusion with Oso, another Washington settlement.[68]

Although mining occurred in the area in the 1870s and 1880s, the settlement did not grow spectacularly. However, by 1891 Oroville's first store had been built, and after that the town grew until it had more than twenty saloons. A 100-ton capacity cyanide plant was built north of town. It was operated by a sixty-horsepower engine and supplied by a 400-foot cable tramway.[69]

Mining and quarrying have never totally died out in the area, as Epsom salts, gold, silver, lead, arsenic, clay, and limestone have been found in paying quantities.

Ravensdale clings to life northeast of Auburn.

The town was a transportation center for the mines, being on the main line of the Northern Pacific Railroad.

It is not known when mining began in the area, but it is known that in 1915 a mining explosion ripped underground, killing thirty-one miners.[70] It was one of the worst mining disasters in state mining history.[71]

Today lumbering and agriculture sustain this former coal-mining settlement, which was once described as being "built along a fluffy green hill which hovers above a gullied flat."

The boarded up school at Ravensdale.

Republic still continues as the center of the most consistent gold-producing district in Washington.

Prospecting began in the area in 1896. John Welty is credited with making the first known gold discovery on February 20, 1896, on sleepy Granite Creek.

Republic burgeoned, and by 1900 was ranked sixth in population among eastern Washington cities.[72] It gloried in having twenty-eight saloons and two[73] dance halls. A railroad was completed between Republic and Grand Forks, British Columbia, in 1902, but because it was unprofitable, it folded later that same year. The railroad was derisively termed the "Hot Air Line" by its detractors, who thought it would never be completed.

The fortunes of Republic yo-yoed from boom to bust.

Gold shipments were made from the settlement until 1901, when the district temporarily closed. But with the coming of the "Hot Air Line" (later sold to the Great Northern), mining activity was resumed, for ores could now profitably be shipped to Pacific Coast smelters.

Deposits discovered in 1909 increased the tempo of mining activities, which continued through 1928. It was an up-and-down situation from 1928 through World War II, when the Knob Hill mine established itself as the largest and most consistent producer—actually the third most productive lode gold mine in the nation.[74]

Republic, Washington — *Courtesy Eastern Washington State Historical Society.*

A view of Republic taken about 1902 from a hill
north of town — *From William C. Brown papers,
Washington State University Library.*

Head frame and hoist house, Surprise mine at Republic — *Washington State University Library.*

Knob Hill mine at Republic — *Washington State University Library.*

W. C. Brown about 1900 near West Fork south of
Republic — *Washington State University Library.*

Settlement of the area that was to become **Rogersburg** probably began in 1860, when, according to legend, three men beached their canoes on the bar of Shovel Creek, which empties into the Snake River. They reportedly found a pailful of gold nuggets in half a day of prospecting.

Short of supplies, the three cached their gold and journeyed to Walla Walla, where one of them was killed, one died of natural causes, and the third disappeared.

For years prospectors tramped to the alleged site of the buried treasure and the rich gravels. In time a town grew up to satisfy their needs. It was designated Rogersburg, and it swelled and contracted in response to the mining activities surrounding it.

Today the village at the junction of the Snake and Grande Ronde rivers has been wiped from the postal records and highway maps.

Roslyn is neither dead nor quite dying, but has played a significant role in the history of Washington coal mining.

The Northern Pacific Railroad began coal mining operations in the Roslyn region[75] in 1886. About 500 laborers worked there at one time, including blacks, who were imported in 1888 to break a strike.

Major mine disasters struck Roslyn in May 1892,[76] when forty-five men were killed in the state's worst coal mine disaster, and in October 1909, when ten miners died.

Roslyn has a cosmopolitan atmosphere, and several European traditions are perpetuated there. As late as World War II, it was a custom of men of Slavic descent to propose marriage on bended knee. According to tradition, if the woman said "no," the rejected suitor would buy a keg of beer in which he and his friends might drown his sorrow, but if the lady said "yes," the Romeo's wedding expenses would be paid by his companions.

Shaft ruins from the October 3, 1909 disaster at Roslyn — *Washington State University Library.*

40

"Upper" Roslyn — *Washington State University Library.*

"Lower" Roslyn — *Washington State University Library.*

A portrait of Roslyn on an early Sunday morning.

Ruby was established northwest of Conconully in 1886. The town was incorporated August 23, 1890[77] and served fleetingly as Okanogan County's first seat of government. At one time Ruby was the only incorporated town in Okanogan County.[78]

The discoverers of the Ruby mine sold it to Jonathan Bourne Jr., United States senator from Portland, Oregon. Bourne and other investors bought several mines and installed a concentrating plant to treat the ores, along with a mile-long cable bucket that ran from the First Thought mine to Ruby. It ran spasmodically in 1892 and 1893 but then stopped for good.

At one time, miners at the Bourne properties made an attempt to secure a pay raise. They failed, and in retaliation they shot out all the front windows of the hotel where Jonathan Bourne was staying.

In one edition, the *Ruby Miner* proudly signalled that Ruby was out of debt and had money in the treasury. Actually, the treasury was not very secure. The county *did* have money—$1,800 in cash. However, because there were no safe storage places, the county treasurer cached the money in a baking tin and buried it on his ranch.[79]

The crash of 1893 was responsible for the closing of mines—one by one. By 1896 only a few diehards remained. A fire in 1900 leveled most of the structures that had not previously been torn down by area residents. The settlement was deserted in 1899.[80] Today there is not a building standing in this once hell-roarin', adamantine former county seat town.

The Old Ruby Quartz Mill. Picture taken in about 1895 after mill was shut down. Location is about one-half mile down Salmon Creek from center of Old Ruby City. The bridge showing is across Salmon Creek on the old road — *From William C. Brown papers, Washington State University Library.*

46

Sehome was one of several Bellingham Bay towns through which gold seekers impetuously rushed on their way to the new discoveries in the Fraser River gold fields. But the settlement was also a coal mining town; in 1873 the Sehome mine was fairly prosperous. Indian laborers were employed by the company to prospect for coal in the area south of Sehome. Chinese miners were employed in the mines, which added to the "cosmopolitan" atmosphere of the settlement.

All houses were company owned, were neatly fenced, and had large, well-kept gardens. The company operated a fleet of three ships—the *Germania,* the *Lookout,* and the *Amethyst.*

In November 1877[81] the Sehome mine was closed. The miners scattered, save for a few caretakers.

Coal miners also lived at *Blue Canyon.* Fred Zobrist located a homestead there in 1886, but mining activities did not get a full impetus until 1891 when James F. Wardner, for whom Wardner, Idaho, and Wardner, British Columbia, were named, bought coal claims in the area. Upon a visit to the properties located up a mountainside, Wardner noted the haunting, transitory bluish tinge of a misty day and named the mine and the town **Blue Canyon.**

A coal mine explosion in Blue Canyon on April 8, 1895 killed twenty-three men. The mine—opened in 1855—was operated spasmodically until 1920, when it was closed permanently.

Glacier was another Whatcom County coal mining town. Anthracite was mined there.

The Diamond Creek Coal Company operated a mine at **Maple Falls. Kendall,** a limestone quarry town, was three miles west of Maple Falls. It was named for Carthage Kendall, who, with a man named Chapman, were the first homesteaders in the north fork area of the Nooksack in 1884.

Deserted, solitary **Sheridan,** northeast of Wauconda, is a mystery mining camp.

When it was born and when it died are not known.

The town's remains hint that it was a company town, with a stable, company offices, and living quarters and a majestic hotel which may never have been occupied. The upper floor of the structure was meant to be a dance hall. It had a walk-out veranda, and below the veranda was a boardwalk leading into a lower level floor. Weis speculates that the reason the hotel was never lived in was because no windows had been cut in either the sides or upper floors of the structure, and that "no sane man would live in a flammable building without an avenue of escape."[83] It seems reasonable to guess that the short-lived mining camp was deserted before the windows were cut and framed.

Maybe some day the facts will be known. But perhaps part of the fun of "ghost towning" is that much room is left for speculation.

The lichen has apparently taken a "likin' " to these cabin logs at Sheridan.

A few people still live at Sheridan, but not here.

Silver Creek and **Silver City** were located in Snohomish County, although historical records of the county are incomplete concerning the two settlements.

Records show that at a miners' meeting at Silver Creek in October 1874 the following laws were drawn up to govern the mining district:

Law I. The name of this mining district shall hereafter be known as the Skykomish Mining District and shall be bounded as follows: Commencing at the junction of the Skykomish and Sultan rivers, thence in an easterly direction along the Cady trail, to the summit of the Cascade range of mountains, thence north along the summit of said range to the headwaters of the middle fork of the Sultan River, thence down the Sultan River to the place of beginning.

Law II. The mining act of the Congress of the United States approved May 10, 1872, is hereby adopted as the laws of this district.

Law III. The posting of notices for claiming mineral ground will be deemed sufficient for holding said claims for twenty days without recording, providing that the parties posting such notices shall not be entitled to a renewal of said notice.

Law IV. All persons posting claims in the district must be present at the time of the location of said claims.

Law V. For the purpose of changing or remodeling the laws of the district, two-thirds of the mine owners of the district may notify the Recorder in writing that a meeting for that purpose will be called, upon which notice the Recorder will post notices in at least three conspicuous places in Snohomish County giving thirty days' notice of said meeting.

Law VI. The term of the office of the Recorder for the district shall be two years, and until his successor is elected.

Law VII. Upon the election of the Recorder his predecessor shall turn over all books and papers pertaining to the office.

Law VIII. The fees of the Recorder shall be as follows: for each 100 feet on a quartz claim 50 cents; for every placer claim located $2.50; for the recording of deeds or transfers $5.00.

Law IX. A copy of the above laws and all laws made in the district must be placed upon record in the office of the County Auditor of Snohomish County.

James McFarlane was elected Recorder for two years.

> Jay G. Kelley, president
> H. L. Pike, secretary[84]

One scrap of information about Silver Creek indicates that "when the fall in the price of silver caused depression in mining . . . the camp [Silver Creek] was almost deserted, and many of the earlier locations were abandoned."[85]

The records indicate that the Silver City (and Mineral City) booms played an important part in the early history of Snohomish County, but that "during the decade of the eighties were not very active, except for relocations and minor transfers."[86]

Depopulated **Silverton** was a gold, silver, and copper producing town.

The camp was located on the Everett & Monte Cristo Railroad fifty miles from Everett. This location gave Silverton a decided advantage as a mine transportation center. The smelter in Everett was fifty-four miles away, that in Tacoma, 128 miles.[87]

It has been estimated that a circle drawn seven miles around Silverton would include all of the principal mining properties of the Silverton mining district.[88]

First discoveries were made in 1891.

Initially called Independence, the name "Silverton" was adopted for the fledgling settlement when the Stillaquamish mining district was organized on August 26, 1891. That winter a townsite was officially established. Later that same year a pack trail was hacked out to Hartford. It was also during 1891 that a wagon road had been constructed, and a railroad almost reached town.

One of the earliest known miners' unions was organized at Silverton in 1893.

However, by about 1910 ore shipments stopped and were never resumed.

The most impressive structure in Silverton, high in the misty clouds.

Silverton in 1906 — *Photography Collection, Suzzallo Library, University of Washington.*

Contrary to what the name might suggest, **Spiketon** was not a railroad town. It began as a sawmill town about 1891 near Buckley. Later a shingle mill was built at the site. The settlement was first known as Pittsburg, as was the mine located near town (the first records of mining date to 1891). On September 7, 1910, the name was changed to Spiketon for D. C. Spike, who had bought the land for mining purposes.

In 1913 there were eight or nine companies producing coal in the area, and perhaps because of them the town name was destined to be changed two more times.

In 1916 the American Coal Company leased the Spiketon mining properties to the South Willis Coal Company, and that year the name was changed to Morristown. Records indicate that the Black Carbon Coal Company took over after the South Willis Coal Company, and somewhere during this tenure the name was changed to Black Carbon. However, during 1928–29 the company ceased mining operations, and Black Carbon, nee Morristown, nee Spiketon, nee Pittsburg, ceased to exist except for some crumbling foundations. Why the town has gone down in dusty history as Spiketon rather than as one of its other monickers is not clear.

Sultan has a long, varied history. The community, located at the confluence of the Sultan and Skykomish rivers, has been described as being "at the foot of the Sultan Basin, a stream whose golden sands have been the lure of many a prospector."[89] It was named for Chief Tseul-tud of the Skykomish tribe.

The first placer strikes occurred in 1870 along the Sultan River. Yet another strike in 1878 touched off more mining furor in the area. Chinese were among the early miners working along the Sultan River, named for the Indian "Sultan John."

In 1880 John Nailor and his Indian wife took a claim at the mouth of the Sultan River, where he set up a way station. Here, "some sort of entertainment could be had for man and beast."[90]

A successful petition was submitted to post office officials in 1885 that the settlement on the Sultan be named Sultan City. John Nailor was the first postmaster.

Another burst of mining activity took place in 1887. In 1891, railroad building was at its height, and Sultan City was made a supply point. In 1888 small river steamers reached Sultan.

A $2,500 schoolhouse was built in 1892, the same year the Bank of Sultan was established. It was also the year of Sultan City's first recorded homicide. In May 1892 George Briton got drunk in the Campbell and O'Leary saloon. Campbell shot Briton, but in the ways of frontier "justice," "Briton forgave Campbell just before he died, so there was no conviction."[91]

The word "City" was dropped from the town's monicker by postal authorities in 1894, and the city was officially incorporated as "Sultan" on June 10, 1905.

A diversity of commercial activities have kept Sultan alive. Today it is a healthy, stable community on Highway 2 southeast of Everett.

Sulton in 1892, seen from across the Snohomish River — *Photography Collection, Suzzallo Library, University of Washington.*

The sign at the Logger's Inn at Sultan proclaims it to be the "oldest in the West."

Sumas was probably founded in July 1858[92] during the first gold rush in the area along Sarr Creek.

In 1882 Sumas was described as "still but a mosquito-breeding swamp."[93]

The camp was nurtured because it lay in the path of the prospectors who wended their way overland along an Indian trail through the Sumas Valley to the rough upper Fraser River country.

Today the settlement serves as a port of entry for the United States Customs Service.

Swauk Prairie was contemporary with, and in close proximity to, Liberty.

But while Liberty has lived on, Swauk Prairie is dead—R.I.P.

Taylor blossomed as the center of a clay products industry about seven miles east of Maple Valley. By 1889, 700 people lived there. In 1892 the Puget Sound Fire Clay Company was purchased by the Denny Clay Company, which also branched out into coal mining. But coal mining operations were slowed by a strike in 1922 and were completely closed down in 1928.

But eventually even the clay mining ceased. Plant dismantling began in 1946, and the last kiln was fired in June 1947. The fate of Taylor was sealed that same year, when the Seattle water department was given permission to include the townsite in the Cedar River watershed. Apparently the townsite was inundated as a result.

Trinity is strung along bubbly Phelps Creek in the Cascades.

It is not known what precious metals were found by prospectors, but initially it was probably gold. Later, about 1900, copper was found. But not until 1914 was the village platted by the Royal Development Company, and a mess hall, commissary, rooming houses, and other structures typical of a company town built.

But the copper veins pinched out and the mine closed, throwing about 275 men out of work.

The settlement pretty much stands as an example of one of Washington's best deserted ghost towns.

Wilkeson was located in 1875 about thirty miles southeast of Tacoma. The town was named for Samuel Wilkeson, secretary of the Northern Pacific Railroad, which built a branch line to the town in 1876[94] or 1877.[95] It was not until March 31, 1891 that the town plat was filed.

The town's population seems to have peaked at about 450 in 1891.

Wilkeson's epitaph might well read, "In the heart of what was once a rich coal-producing region, Wilkeson . . . has been transformed into a ghost community by the depletion of its coal deposits and forests."[96] Following short-lived coal mining and lumbering ventures, the commerce of Wilkeson turned to sandstone quarrying. As one observer put it, "The excitement was all over by 1900 and the place has settled quietly back since then."[97]

Pittsburgh is another Pierce County ghost town where coal was once produced.[98]

The "curiosity shop" on the edge of Wilkeson.

There were (and are) other interesting settlements in Washington, most of which were not mining camps. However, their histories and lore are of significance, and in many instances they sport physical memorabilia too enticing to neglect when experienced with a camera in hand.

These places deserve consideration and are given it as follows.

Office of the Northwest Talc and Magnesium Company at Clear Lake.

Altoona, in Wahkiakum County, is a grouping of remnants of a fishing and canning village.

Clearlake (Clear Lake) is northeast of Mt. Vernon, in Skagit County. Although not really a ghost town, Clearlake is just the kind of place that is enticing for taking photographs.

Curlew is a picturesque Ferry County town a dozen or so miles below the Canadian border.

Danville is a border checkpoint on Highway 21 just below the Canadian border. The town's environs are quite ghostly, retaining vestiges of more prosperous times.

Danville.

Remains of the Peter Nelson Company Mercantile at Danville.

Frances was a Centralia-Chehalis-area town that sprouted up in southwestern Washington. The most impressive legacy of earlier days in the imposing Peoples Store.

Frances.

Frankfort, in Pacific County, was perhaps named for two promoters with the first names of Frank. These two men laid out a townsite in 1890. A handful of people still call the isolated settlement "home."

Havillah came into being southeast of Oroville. It was probably founded in 1903 — at least, that is when Martin Schweikert built a gristmill and store and sold his flour called "Gold Sheaf." The flour mill was later converted to a schoolhouse, which still stands.

Home came into being north of Olympia as a colony of "free spirits" intent on attaining the ultimate in freedom. The settlement on Joe's Bay did not last very long in that capacity, and today the town is a quiet village.

Knappton, on Gray's Bay along the Columbia River, was first called Cementville, and later Knappton (in 1871) for its first postmaster, Jabez Knapp. A raging fire in 1941 almost killed the town, and in 1943 the post office closed.

A few houses remain today, as well as the old Knappton quarantine station, which for more than half a century served as a place where immigrants were detained by the United States Public Health Service if suspected of carrying communicable diseases.

Malo is on Highway 21 north of Republic, in northeastern Washington. The town is surrounded by the Colville National Forest. Several attractive structures remain.

Malo.

Methow is northwest of Bridgeport, in Okanogan County. The pleasant town is on the edge of the Wenatchee National Forest on Highway 153. Almost 400 people call it home.

Methow.

Part of the display at the Molson museum.

Molson is east and slightly north of Oroville, just below the Canadian border. The town was originally a mining camp, but evolved into an agricultural community. The camp, founded in 1900, was named for mine investor John Molson, who, so the story goes, never visited the place.[99]

Pillar Rock is in Wahkiakum County, near Altoona. Old wharves and several deserted structures dot the landscape.

Port Blakeley grew up as a sawmill town in Kitsap County. The Port Blakeley mill may have been the largest in the world — 400,000 board feet of lumber were cut each day by 1,200 men.[100] A few ferry commuters to Seattle and others call the place home, but most of original Port Blakeley is gone.

Riverside is north of Omak in Okanogan County. The town was primarily a transportation center, but when the railroad bypassed Riverside in 1914, the future of the town became doubtful. It still survives.

Ronald is a couple of miles from Roslyn, in Kittitas County. Extensive mine buildings remain from the days when Ronald's mines furnished coal for trains crossing the Cascade Mountains.

Extant **Skamokawa** in Wahkiakum County is still alive. The one-time riverboat stop retains many vestiges of the past, including several false-fronted buildings.

Notes

1. A. H. Koschmann and M. H. Bergendahl, *Principal Gold-Producing Districts of the United States*, U.S. Geological Survey Professional Paper 610, U.S. Government Printing Office, Washington, D.C., 1968, p. 216.
2. *Ibid.* The Knob Hill mine in the Republic district ranks third among lode gold producing mines, while the Gold King mine in the Wenatchee district ranks tenth.
3. Troy ounces are used in the measurement of gold and silver. One troy ounce equals 1,097 "regular" ounces avoirdupois. The term is derived from the city of Troyes, on the Seine River in France.
4. Koschmann and Bergendahl, p. 216.
5. Statistics referred to in Rodman Wilson Paul, *Mining Frontiers of the Far West*, Holt, Rinehart and Winston, New York, 1963, p. 149.
6. Joseph Gaston, *The Centennial History of Oregon*, Vol. I, The S. J. Clarke Publishing Company, Chicago, 1912, p. 491.
7. T. A. Rickard, *A History of American Mining*, McGraw-Hill, New York, 1932, p. 316.
8. Percival R. Jeffcott, *Chichaco and Sourdough*, Pioneer Printing Company, Bellingham, Washington, 1963, p. 5.
9. *Seattle Times*, Dec. 17, 1967.
10. Other coal-producing towns in King County include RENTON and the ghost towns of NEWCASTLE, DURHAM, FRANKLIN, GILMAN, and DAVILLE.
11. See U.S. Bureau of Mines Bulletin 586, *Historical Summary of Coal-Mine Explosions in the United States, 1810-1958*, U.S. Government Printing Office, Washington, D.C., pp. 22–23.
12. *Washington*, Washington Writers' Project (W.P.A.), American Guide Series, Binfords and Mort, Portland, 1941, p. 349; hereafter referred to simply as *Washington*. A visit in 1974 left the impression that the scene was generally unchanged from 1941, but no cows were observed in the streets.
13. Norman Weis, *Ghost Towns of the Northwest*, Caxton Printers, Caldwell, Idaho, 1971, p. 85 indicates that the date may have been 1854.
14. L. K. Hodges (ed.), *Mining in the Pacific Northwest*, The Post-Intelligencer, Seattle, Washington, 1897 (reproduced by the Shorey Book Store, Seattle, 1967), p. 7, calls it Penhustin Creek.
15. Hodges, p. 71 and Koschmann and Bergendahl, p. 256.
16. Muriel Sibell Wolle, *The Bonanza Trail*, University of Indiana Press, Bloomington, 1953, pp. 284–85.
17. Hodges, p. 72.
18. Wolle, p. 285, and Weis, p. 85; but Weis finds the figure suspect.
19. Koschmann and Bergendahl, p. 257.
20. Weis, p. 114.
21. Weis, p. 106.
22. *Tacoma News Tribune and Sunday Ledger*, Oct. 14, 1962.
23. Bureau of Mines Bulletin 586, p. 123.
24. *Washington*, p. 352.
25. *History of the Big Bend Country*, Western Historical Company, Spokane, 1904, p. 195.
26. Hodges, map on p. 115.
27. *Washington*, p. 451.
28. Weis, p. 103.
29. Apparently gold was discovered near what became Conconully in 1871, according to Koschmann and Bergendahl, p. 259; but until 1886, this was Indian land forbidden to whites.
30. An honor it lost in 1915.
31. According to some sources, "Conconully" means "evil spirit."
32. Hodges, p. 94.
33. *History of Big Bend Country*, p. 187.
34. Hodges, p. 97.
35. *The Seattle Times*, June 27, 1971, reports discovery year as 1890, but this date is suspect.

36. There may have been a BARBER CAMP or BARBER AND HOAG CAMP about two miles above Union City, according to Jeffcott, pp. 101 and 103.

37. Lancaster Pollard, *A History of the State of Washington*, Vol. II, The American Historical Society, New York, 1937, p. 141.

38. *Washington*, p. 431.

39. William Whitfield (ed.), *History of Snohomish County*, Vol. I, Pioneer Historical Publishing Company, Chicago, 1926, p. 610.

40. *Ibid.*, p. 611.

41. *Ibid.*, p. 724. As an example of the economic health of the town, Whitfield reports that in 1895 the daily payroll at the Index granite quarry was $100.

42. Lambert Florin, *Western Ghost Towns*, Superior Publishing Company, Seattle, 1961, p. 24.

43. Weis, p. 80, says that the discovery was in 1867 and that Goodwin found the nugget when he kicked over some rocks to make it easier to get some cooking water.

44. Hodges, p. 67. Wolle, p. 284, says it was worth "a few cents."

45. Hodges, p. 67. Wolle, p. 286, says "Nuggets worth from $20 to $1,120 were not infrequently taken from the Swauk."

46. *Washington*, p. 316.

47. *Seattle Times*, Aug. 5, 1968.

48. *Tacoma News Tribune*, March 29, 1964.

49. Lottie Roeder Roth (ed.), *History of Whatcom County*, Vol. I, Pioneer Historical Publishing Company, Chicago, 1926, p. 340.

50. *Ibid.*

51. *Ibid.*, p. 341.

52. Hodges, p. 96.

53. Lambert Florin, *Ghost Town Trails*, Superior Publishing Company, Seattle, 1963, p. 56.

54. Hodges, p. 54.

55. "Ghost Towns and Forts of Washington," (a map), The Christiansens, Sprague, Washington, n.d.

56. W. P. Bonney, *History of Pierce County*, Pioneer Historical Publishing Company, Chicago, Vol. I, 1927, p. 509.

57. Although the Everett-Monte Cristo distance is about 40 miles, the Everett-Monte Cristo Railroad line stretched 63 miles between the two points. The line was begun in spring 1892 and completed in August 1893 (*Seattle Post-Intelligencer*, Dec. 27, 1964.) Stewart Holbrook, in *Far Corner*, Ballantine Books, New York, 1952, p. 113, is somewhat derisive of the Rockefeller mine at Monte Cristo. He indicates that the camp was named for the Alexander Dumas novel and states, "The novel was great fiction. So was the mine. I do not know how much the Frenchman made from his novel. I do not know how much the Rockefellers got from the mine which, with excellent judgment, they abandoned after their experts had given the first few loads of ore a thorough working-over at the smelter."

58. The "usual" vigilante symbol was 3-7-77.

59. Wolle, p. 292.

60. Koschmann and Bergendahl, p. 261.

61. Florin, *Ghost Town Trails*, p. 52.

62. Lambert Florin, in *Ghost Town Album*, Superior Publishing Company, Seattle, 1962, p. 139 indicates that the year was 1897.

63. *Ibid.;* he indicates that it was owned by the Northport Smelting and Refining Company.

64. Hodges, p. 111.

65. That would have been the Spokane Falls and Northern Railroad.

66. Hult, p. 165.

67. Wolle, p. 274.

68. Probably this was in 1896, according to Hodges, p. 102.

69. It's possible Oroville was built on or near an early mining camp site known as CHOPAKA CITY.

70. An account of the explosion and its aftermath appears in the U.S. Bureau of Mines Bulletin 586, p. 78.

71. The largest Washington coal mine explosion in terms of loss of human life was the May 10, 1892 disaster at Roslyn, in which 45 lives were lost.

72. Other mining camps in the vicinity included OLD WAUCONDA and CURLEW.

73. Florin, in *Ghost Town Album*, indicates there may have been six dance halls (p. 136).

74. Koschmann and Bergendahl, p. 258.

75. The Northern Pacific also was responsible for establishing nearby RONALD, site of the old Number 3 stope of the Roslyn field, where coal was mined for trains crossing the Cascade Mountains.
76. The combination of the mine disaster and the subsequent robbery of the Ben E. Snipes bank by members of Butch Cassidy's "Wild Bunch," brought the whole Snipes empire to ruin. See Washington State University Friends of the Library *Record,* Volume 32 (1972), pp. 27–72, for details.
77. *Wenatchee Daily World,* August 28, 1923.
78. Donald E. Bower, *Ghost Towns and Back Roads,* Stackpole Books, Harrisburg, Pennsylvania, 1971, p. 194.
79. Wolle, p. 278.
80. *Wenatchee Daily World,* March 3, 1963.
81. Jeffcott, p. 11, says the mine was closed in 1878.
82. Roth, p. 941.
83. Weis, p. 124.
84. Reproduced from Whitfield, p. 721.
85. Hodges, p. 26.
86. Whitfield, p. 721.
87. Hodges, p. 17.
88. *Ibid.*
89. Whitfield, p. 600.
90. *Ibid.*
91. *Ibid.,* p. 604.
92. The first claim may not have been staked until 1887, says Jeffcott, p. 61.
93. *Ibid.,* p. 64.
94. *Washington,* p. 351.
95. Bonney, p. 385.
96. *Washington,* p. 351.
97. Florin, *Western Ghost Towns,* p. 31.
98. Hodges, p. 10.
99. Weis, p. 94.
100. Florin, p. 141.

Oregon

Union

Silverton • Milford

Homestead

Cornucopia
Sanger
Copperfield
Sparta

Shaniko

Granite • Bourne
Sumpter
Greenhorn •
Galena • Susanville • Auburn
Ashwood • Horse Heaven

Whitney
Austin Bonanza

Quartzville

Mitchell

Prairie City
Antone • Bakeoven • Marysville Unity Malheur City
Howard • Canyon City

Beulah

Drewsey

Scottsburg

Bohemia

Empire City
• Libby
• Henryville

• Riverton
Bandon

• Powers

Golden •
• Greenback
• Placer

Gold Beach

• Gold Hill

• Jacksonville
Kerby • • Applegate
• Browntown
Waldo • • Althouse

Allentown sprang up near the mouth of Allen Gulch, in the Waldo area, but exactly when is not known. Gold discoveries had been made in the region as early as 1853.

Whatever the discovery year, miners held a meeting during the approach of the first winter and determined that not all could stay at the camp because of insufficient provisions.

One of the men who was forced to leave camped at nearby Butcher Gulch, where he wintered well on wild game. He visited Allentown in February and found many miners starving. He provided them with a steady supply of meat. Not only did he find game; he found gold. Not anxious to share both gold and meat with his fellow miners, the exile managed to keep his secret by outfoxing the men who hoped to follow him as he returned to his mine from Allentown. His modus operandi was to either pretend to get drunk and pass out, or wait until the last man drank himself into oblivion and then leave for his diggings.

A church was built at Allentown in the 1860s, and Father F. X. Blanchard conducted services there.[1] He was popular with the miners, for he spoke their colorful language, smoked a pipe, and shared his whisky.

Like moles, the miners dug to bedrock along creeks and gulches. In the mid-1870s (and again around the turn of the century) "hydraulic giants" were turned loose to flush the deep gravels and expose the precious metals.

But then the gold was gone, and so was Allentown.

Althouse was one of several gold mining camps that grew up in southern Josephine County. It was probably named for John and Philip Althouse.[2]

The settlement was overshadowed by Waldo, Oregon's first gold discovery site, but it shared the state's first mining code, which stated that "the miners of Waldo and Althouse in Oregon Territory, being in convention assembled for the purpose of making rules and regulations to govern this camp," set forth four brief resolutions to define the code. The code established what should be the claim on the bed of a creek extending to high water on each side and what should constitute a bank or bar claim. It specified that after five days a claim would be forfeited or "jumpable" if not worked when "workable," that all disputes arising from mining claims should be settled by arbitration, and that the arbitrator's decisions would be final.[3]

The site of **Antone**, east of Mitchell, consists of only a road marker.

In mining history, Antone is remembered as being the western terminus of a dike, or vein, of gold-bearing rock that was thought to run from there through Canyon City, Prairie City, Auburn, Whitman, Sumpter, Cornucopia, and Copperfield, into Idaho through Cuprum, from there on to Riggins, and then to its end in the almost-disappeared ghost town of Florence.

This is Antone — ALL of it.

A mailbox near Antone.

Applegate has been not only a mining community, but also a fruit-growing and lumbering town.

The settlement was named for Jesse and Lindsay Applegate.[4]

Some rich strikes were made in the gravels near Applegate. Legend relates that Chiny Linn, a Chinese, removed more than $2 million in gold from his claim, but the tale seems unlikely due to the fact that the average annual gold production in the entire Josephine County mining district between 1852 and 1900 was probably only about $450,000.[5]

The short-lived mining camps of **Willow Springs, Pleasant Creek, Murphy,** and **Sterlingville** sprang up in the area, but little is known of their histories.

Jesse Applegate — *Oregon Historical Society.*

Lindsay Applegate — *Oregon Historical Society.*

An overburdened mailbox post at Applegate.

Ashwood grew up on Trout Creek, northeast of Madras, in the 1870s.[6]

Sometime in the geological history of the area, lava flows and volcanic ash formed nearby Ash Butte. When the post office was established in the camp in 1898, part of the name of the first postmaster—Whitfield T. Wood—was combined with part of Ash Butte's name to form "Ashwood."

Some consider the founder of Ashwood to have been Thomas J. Brown, who, when herding sheep in a gulch leading into Trout Creek, found gold and silver-bearing quartz deposits.[7] The settlement that grew up a couple of miles from the mine (the Oregon King) became Ashwood.

As the mines failed, Ashwood's population dwindled. Today several remaining original structures hint of the town's history as a gold and mercury-mining and cattle-raising settlement.

A jerry-build structure at Ashwood.

A scene near the site of Auburn.

Auburn, located near Baker in north central Oregon, was the site of the first gold rush (1861) in the eastern part of the state. Area gold fields were discovered in Griffin Gulch[8] by Henry Griffin and David Little-field. The early settlers built log cabins and a blockhouse as protection against Indian raids. Auburn grew to a population of about 5,000 between 1862 and 1864 and became the state's second largest city. By act of the Oregon legislature, on September 22, 1862, the town became the county seat. The single long street along which Auburn was laid out was built July 13, 1862 "from Freezeout Gulch to Blue Canyon," as the saying went.

A number of Chinese came to Auburn to operate laundries, restaurants, and gambling houses and to seek gold left by white men. In some respects, the Chinese[9] were welcome in Auburn for financial reasons. The Auburn Canal Company's ditch brought water to area gulches for twenty-five cents per miners' inch, [10] but the price was considered exorbitant. By inviting the Chinese to share the water, the miners got theirs at a reduced "wholesale" price.

In 1867 Auburn began to die as its restless citizens swarmed to the newly discovered gold fields in Idaho. The following year the county seat was moved to Baker, and Auburn withered to nothing but graves. Three graveyards mark the site—one for whites, two for Chinese. However, as one publication laments, "One of the latter was washed away in a 'second washing' for gold."[11]

Auburn in 1861 — *Oregon Historical Society.*

One of the first hangings in Auburn was that of a miner, French Pete, who was convicted of poisoning a fellow miner[12] by adding strychnine to his partner's flour. A historian writes of the event: "Being tried before an extemporaneous judge and jury, he was found guilty and executed on the spot in order to save the citizens the trouble and expense of conveying him to Dalles City, 250 miles away, for trial."[13]

Austin sprang up midway between Dixie and Blue Mountain passes as a supply town for area mines.

The town still exists, exuding memories of the heyday years, when at one time the population rose to 5,000.[14]

An old roadhouse and stage station was established at the site by a Mrs. Newton, and the settlement was first called Newton's Station. The name was changed when Minor Austin bought the buildings.

Bakeoven was not a mining town, but it is tied in with Oregon mining because it was founded by Joseph H. Sherar, who was packing supplies to the miners at Canyon City in 1862 when he founded the settlement.

It seems that one evening in 1862 Sherar and his German cook stopped at the Bakeoven spring to have dinner.

An abandoned service station at Austin.

While Sherar tended to other camping duties, the cook built a clay stove with an oven for baking bread. As one writer puts it, "Not only could they use the oven and fireplace, but other packers and miners were welcome to do so. In that manner and for that reason, the miners and pack train operators and later the freight wagon operators came to know and call the place Bake Oven, because there was a place at that spring [Bakeoven spring] to bake bread."[15]

In 1872 the area became the Bakeoven Stage Station. In 1875 a post office was established, with Mrs. Tom Burgess functioning as first postmistress, storekeeper, and innkeeper.

In 1901 the railroad bypassed Bakeoven, and the town began to die. The post office was closed in 1918. The townsite now is part of a 90,000-acre ranch.

The still-extant settlement of **Bandon** was once a coal mining town.

In 1852 a man named Henry H. Baldwin, along with the shipwrecked crew of the *Captain Lincoln,* crossed the area that was to encompass Bandon while en route to Port Orford. Baldwin liked the region and later returned as a settler. He persuaded a friend, George Bennet of Bandon, Ireland, to join him. It is not certain when the settlement was named Bandon. An early issue of the *Roseburg Review* states, "Although the precinct has been named Bandon since 1874, the congregation of houses and other buildings that constitute the town was called Averhill until 1889."

What does seem clear is that the townsite of what was to become Bandon was "taken up" in 1853, "not for the gold that glittered in the front of it . . . but because of a convenient place for a ferry, and from its admirable position for commercial purposes."[16]

And Bandon has lived on since, as a sawmill town, as a shipyard center, then as the site of a woolen mill, and currently as a tourist center. At one time Bandon also served as the nucleus of a coal mining venture of the Bandon Block Coal Company, which employed blacks[17] in the mines. The coal was shipped by steamboat to San Francisco.

Beaver Hill was a Coos County coal mining town near the headwaters of Beaver Slough.

Beaver Hill achieved technical classification as a city on January 11, 1896, with all but one of its eighty-five registered voters voting for the incorporation.

Beaver Hill was a company town, featuring a large store, a bunkhouse, a cook house, and many miners' dwellings. Mail was brought to town on the company train and distributed in the company store. This may account for the fact that the town never officially had a post office. As one writer claims, "No other incorporated city in this area lived through three decades without having an established post office."[18]

About 1920 the coal mine was closed, and half a dozen years later only sixteen voters could be found to vote for disincorporation of the hamlet.

Today the town is gone.

Beulah is considered by some to be a mining ghost town because it was near there that Sarah Chambers was buried while traveling along the route taken by an immigrant wagon train, some members of which perhaps discovered the fabled lost Blue Bucket mine, which was supposed to have been "two days westward" from the Beulah area.

Little of Beulah remains, the area having been flooded by the Agency Reservoir years ago.[19]

Bohemia was named for James "Bohemia" Johnson, who discovered gold in the Calapooya mountains between the Willamette and Umpqua rivers in 1863.

Johnson brought out gold that he had extracted from quartz ledges. It was not free milling (i.e., it could not be reduced by crushing and amalgamation; it usually had to be roasted or given chemical treatment), and so little excitement followed until 1891. By 1900 the area was booming. But ten years later it was almost deserted, mainly because the remaining low-grade ores were too expensive to mine and process profitably.

Bonanza, midway between Whitney and Greenhorn along the north fork of the Burnt River, was a gold camp.[20]

Boardinghouses, remnants of a sixty-stamp mill where perhaps up to $2 million worth of gold was processed, and parts of a mine discovered in 1877 can be found.

Remains of ruined buildings dot the townsite.

Bourne was born in 1895,[21] was nurtured by printer's ink for a few years, and died after a short history involving one of Oregon's biggest attempted swindles.

The settlement—founded in the 1870s as a gold camp called Cracker and later renamed in honor of United States Senator Jonathan Bourne—might have grown to a population of 3,000. But it was really only a boom town on paper—newspaper.

In 1900 a press was brought in by wagon, since no railroad existed. Two newspapers were issued by the same firm, one for local consumption, the other for potential investors in the Sampson Company, Ltd. The latter publication was termed by some the "sucker"[22] edition; it gave glowing accounts of imagined rich mineral strikes and fabulous riches.

The Sampson Company "of London, New York and Bourne" fleeced hundreds through the mails. Profits were used for a mansion designed and built in 1906 by J. Wallace White. For years the dazzling white house on the Bourne hillside stood as a monument to what has been termed one of Oregon's most flagrant mining swindles.[23]

By 1906 it was apparent that Bourne was built on dreams, and most people moved away. The few mines that had been producing were closed. The final curtain was rung down on Bourne in 1937 when a cloudburst washed away most of the buildings in town.

A contemporary writer describes the current scene: "Bourne today is a seedy scatter of scarecrow houses strewn over the hills and flats, with loose boards flapping in the banshee winds."[24]

Bourne

Jonathan Bourne —
Oregon Historical Society.

Browntown[25] grew up in extreme southern Josephine County. It was named for Henry H. "Webfoot" Brown, who later became a California newspaper publisher.

Area mines yielded gold, including a nugget supposedly valued at $1,200.[26]

The town's population probably peaked at between 800 and 1,000.[27] Buildings included seven or eight saloons, three dry goods and clothing stores, two bakeries, four or five restaurants and hotels, seven or eight grocery stores, a bowling alley, two or three butcher shops, and three or four blacksmith shops; plus "Two Dance or Fancy houses."

Little remains of the settlement.

Caledonia, on the Isthmus Inlet, was fathered by a nearby coal mine.

No trace of the original town remains, although a few newer houses stand on the original site.

Strictly speaking, the county seat settlement of **Canyon City** is not a ghost town, but it is a ghost of its former self; consequently, it is included in this publication.

The town was born in 1862[28] as a camp that ballooned along Canyon Creek after gold was discovered on Whiskey Flat, a short distance north of the present town, by a party of miners searching for the lost "Blue Bucket" mine.[29] Perhaps as many as 10,000[30] people lived along the single Whiskey Gulch street. It has been estimated that up to $8 million was taken from the Canyon Creek diggings in one decade.[31]

The mining boom busted in the 1870s, but the town did not die.

One of the town's better-known citizens was Cincinnatus Heiner (Joaquin) Miller. Miller and his family settled in Canyon City in 1864. The town's first orchard consisted of trees brought there by Miller and planted at the rear of his cabin. At last report, they continued to bear fruit near the Miller cabin, a still-standing Canyon City attraction.

A ditch—the John Long ditch—provided water from Pine Creek for the miners.[32]

Conflicts were reported between Union and Confederate sympathizers. It has been said that when the Confederate-leaning California miners raised the Confederate flag on Rebel Hill north of the camp on July 4, 1863, the Union-sympathizing Oregon miners stormed the hill and tore down the flag.

The settlement supported a newspaper, but not very well. The *City Journal* was published only seven times. Its masthead significantly read, "Published occasionally."[33] News from Canyon City, however, was sometimes carried in The *Dalles Daily Mountaineer.* For example, Joaquin Miller, in "Canyon City Pickles," his series of letters that appeared in the *Mountaineer,* once described the business activities at Canyon City: "I saw three live merchants, all busy, of course. Bruner was lying on the counter, tickling his cat under the tail with a straw. McNamara was sitting at the breakfast table, picking his nose with a fork. Felsheimer had finished his breakfast and sat at the table quietly paring his toenails with the butter knife. A merchant sold a pair of shoestrings last week and went to his drawer for the change, but the thing had rusted in its place from idleness, and he had to use a crowbar to open it."[34]

Much of original Canyon City was destroyed by fire in 1937.

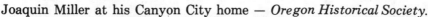

Joaquin Miller at his Canyon City home — *Oregon Historical Society.*

Copperfield is in a mining area, but is considered to have been a railroad town. It was laid out in 1908 to accommodate railroad construction crews and builders of a large power plant.

The town was full of toughs and rowdies, and the Baker County authorities refused to clean it up. Nor did the good citizens of Copperfield get much support from the mayor or city council. The officials either ran saloons or had financial interests in them.[35]

Governor Oswald West finally dispatched his secretary, Fern Hobbs, to Copperfield on New Year's Day 1914 with orders to clean up the town.

Hobbs was accompanied by a national guard colonel, five other national guardsmen, and two state prison guards.

The townsfolk turned out to welcome the "army" sent to save Copperfield from itself. Bunting and flags hung in the streets, and reportedly all saloons were outfitted with pink and white ribbons and flowers.

The secretary strode to the town hall, mounted a platform, and read the governor's orders calling for the resignation of all town officials connected with the saloon business. If they failed to comply, the plucky Hobbs was going to deliver the governor's declaration of martial law, take all weapons, close the saloons, set the torch to all gambling equipment, and get rid of all liquor and saloon fixtures.

The city fathers said "no thanks" to her demands. But the secretary declared martial law, collected all weapons, closed all saloons within eighty minutes, and then took the train out of town, leaving her small army for "mop-up" operations.

A few months later the guardsmen left, and a fire, thought to have been set by an arsonist, burned down most of the town. It was never rebuilt.

Copperfield at the Oxbow Dam site, circa 1910 — *Oregon Historical Society.*

Cornucopia was probably named by miners who had come from Cornucopia, Nevada.

Of the several mines worked in the area, the Union and Companion claims were probably the first, dating back to perhaps 1878.[36]

Most lode mines were not discovered until the 1880s, and Cornucopia's heyday, when its population may have reached 1,000, came between 1884 and 1886. In 1885 a newspaper said that the town sported only one "nice" frame house, tents, cabins, five saloons, a store, two restaurants, a blacksmith shop, a butcher shop, a livery stable, and a lodging house. About 1898 the town-site was moved closer to the mines, but the school, some saloons, and a doctor's office remained at the original site.[37]

In 1895 the Cornucopia Mining Company bought the Union Companion mine (and perhaps changed its name to the Cornucopia mine) and added a twenty-stamp mill. Mine and mill were closed in 1903.

There was a resurgence of mining in 1938 when the Cornucopia Company erected houses, a school, and other structures. But the mines closed in 1941.

Decrepit remnants of structures in the original part of the settlement moulder in the high country around Cornucopia.

Cornucopia, 1887 — *Oregon Historical Society.*

Assay office at Cornucopia — *Patricia Stewart Baker photo collection, Oregon Historical Society.*

Dant is a Johnny-come-lately camp on the Oregon mining scene. First known as Freida when the post office was established there in June 1950, the name was changed December 1, 1950 to Dant.[38] However, the site was first discovered in 1919 by Joseph N. Axfor.[39]

The town was named for the Dant and Russell perlite mine, located nearby.[40]

The perlite in the Dant mine locations may have been caused by a volcano which erupted under Condon Lake; the perlite mines there seem to come from lava flows emanating from the lake.

Drewsey, northeast of Burns in Harney County, was once on the stage route from Vale to Burns.

Abner Robbins built a store there in 1883 and dubbed the settlement "Gouge Eye," after the typical frontier method of settling disputes. Postal authorities refused to adopt the name, and the town ended up being called Drewsey, in honor of Drewsey Miller, daughter of an area rancher.[41]

The town was the scene of activities of cattlemen, gamblers, miners, and a host of adventurers.

Men pose with a threshing machine at Drewsey
— *Oregon Historical Society.*

Drewsey, Oregon

Traces of **Eldorado** are difficult to find. The town was located about two miles northeast of Malheur City. A fort called Eldorado was also situated nearby.

It is not known when the settlement was born, but men from Eldorado discovered the nearby gold camp of Malheur City in 1863.

The *Baker City Bedrock Democrat* of May 13, 1873 reported that "During the day the streets of Eldorado are deserted, all men at work in the tunnels back of town. Great hopes are placed on the benefits to be derived from the 'Big Ditch' under construction by Packwood and Carter; water will be in the ditch in less than ten days. The future of Eldorado looks very bright."

The "Big Ditch" referred to was completed in 1873. The magnificent engineering project stretched for 120[42] miles, from Last Chance Creek of the South Fork of the Burnt River, through Eldorado to Malheur City. The ditch was used to bring water to the mining camps and the diggings, and rafts of logs were floated in it for use in buildings and for timbering at the mines.

The $250,000 "Big Ditch" carried 2,500 miners' inches of water. It was considered to be the West's longest ditch[43] and traces of it can still be found.

Empire City was one of the Coos Bay area camps (including North Bend and Coquille) founded in the Coos Bay coalfields.

The discoveries were made in 1854, and since then the fields have been the most important commercially worked coal sources in the state.

Later, Empire City became known as a lumber milling town. As one observer put it, "the town grew with more promise than achievement through the years,"[44] but it did become a part of the lumber industry in the Coos Bay area, and for its first dozen or so years of existence was the most important city in the Coos Bay area.

Galena

Galena was in the center of an area rich in galena ore. The mines were opened in the 1860s and have been fairly consistent producers since.

The first strikes were probably made in 1862 by a group of tight-lipped miners; but by 1864 the word of the gold discoveries had spread, and soon all potential claims along Elk and Middle Day creeks were staked.

After the first discoveries were exploited, the town began to expire, but during the 1930s dredges clawed at the creek beds and the town revived. By 1943, however, the village was so depopulated that the post office was forced to close.

The peak population of Galena is not known, but one writer believes that at one time 5,000 miners visited Galena to cast votes in an unsuccessful effort to move the county seat to Galena from Canyon City.[45]

Scattered remains mark the site of Galena, where, at last report, one family still lived.

Beach mining probably took place along the Oregon coast as early as 1852. It is estimated that 1,000 miners were washing gold harbored in the sands along the beaches in 1853.[46] However, one of the problems with beach mining was that the gold had been carried from mountains to sea, then washed back to shore and shifted back and forth by waves until it was broken down so finely that much of it could not be seen with the naked eye.

It is not known for certain when gold was discovered in **Gold Beach**,[47] which has lived on although the nearby early mining camps of Whalesburg, Elizabethtown, and Sebastopol have disappeared.

Not much of a wagon road existed to Gold Beach until 1890, when roads led to Crescent City (California) and Coos County. The road was rough and ran from sea level to mountain top. Teams had trouble passing each other. A tale about two teams meeting near Humbug Mountain relates: "It became necessary, not only to unhitch one of the teams, but to unload the wagon, to take off its wheels, uncouple the reachpole, and stack the parts to one side so that the other team and wagon could pass. The first wagon then had to be re-assembled, reloaded, and re-hitched. All this required real team work."[48]

The town has lived on and is today a community of about 2,000.

At or near Gold Beach — *Oregon Historical Society.*

It is unclear when **Golden** became a town, but the post office opened in 1896. Miners may have been in the area before the mid-nineteenth century. It would appear that the white miners left for other "bonanzas," while the Chinese came to the area perhaps in the 1850s. One estimate is that at one time 500 Chinese miners lived along the length of Coyote Creek, near Golden.[49]

White miners returned to the area and ran off the Chinese, then used hydraulic giants to wash away precious gravels along the creek. Perhaps more than 150 people lived along Coyote Creek in 1892. A church, carriage house, and general store were built.

One author uncovered some interesting information about a family in Golden. He writes, "By all reason, they should have named the town 'Ruble City.' The first minister was William Ruble, later replaced by his son, W. N. Ruble. Schuyler Ruble was the first postmaster, and S. C. Ruble was active in the local mining effort. He was the inventor of the Ruble elevator, a device designed to remove unwanted gravel from streambeds. S. C. Ruble also ran the general store. S. C. Ruble and Schuyler Ruble may have been the same person. If so, he was obviously talented and busy."[50]

However, the "long arm of the law" was not in the person of a member of the Ruble clan. Coyote Smith was appointed justice of the peace. But there was not much law to enforce in Golden because there were no saloons, and two churches. A dance hall was built away from town on Wolf Creek, but the former owner said that church members gave him trouble by parading around the dance hall 'Prayin' away the devil.'[51]

Today the small settlement on the Coyote Creek road still consists of the carriage house, general store, and the Golden Community church, built by the Campbellites and later used as a Free Methodist church. Several older structures also remain.

The General Store at Golden.

The Golden Community Church, with a light bulb burning over the entrance.

As early as 1849 the area around **Gold Hill** was known to have gold deposits, but they were not considered to be available in paying quantities.

While gold was not thought to be plentiful, Indians were known to be. So in 1855–56 David N. Birdseye built a log stockade[52] near the mouth of Birdseye Creek, near Gold Hill. The stockade could hold up to 500 persons.

Later, in 1860, the first quartz mill in Jackson County was built at Gold Hill.

The still-existing town has seen mining for limestone and marl[53] as well as for gold.

Miners near Gold Hill — *Southern Oregon Historical Society.*

Gold Hill — *Southern Oregon Historical Society.*

A typical structure at Gold Hill.

Miners arrived at what was to become **Granite** on July 4, 1862. They thought that an appropriate monicker for the fledgling settlement would be "Independence." However, the postal authorities did not want two Oregon settlements with the same name, so in 1878 the name was changed to Granite, for the typical "country" rock[54] found in the area.

The population may have grown to 5,000. For many years an imposing vestige of Granite's past was the ornate thirty-room Grand Hotel. A few years ago it burned to the ground.

Fire and the weight of countless tons of heavy winter snow have slowly taken their toll. Today only one person lives in town, and most of the original buildings are gone.

The main floor of this building in Granite served as saloon, boardinghouse, and community hall. The top floor was a dance hall.

Granite

Greenback apparently grew up around the rich Greenback mine, probably near the turn of the century.

A twenty-stamp mill was built in the area and run by a crew of twenty men, twenty-four hours a day. Cabins and a company store were built, and by 1902 Greenback had a post office. In 1908 the post office was closed.

However, mining operations apparently did not cease in 1908, as a small, modern ball mill has been erected next to the older, original mill. Modern mining operations are carried on spasmodically in the immediate area. Visitors are not welcome.

The sign on the road to Greenback. Such messages should be respected.

Greenhorn was named for two greenhorns from the East who discovered gold in the area. And thereby hangs a tale.

Legend relates that the two greenhorns came to the Blue Mountains of Oregon about 1890. They reportedly walked up to a saloon and asked the barkeeper where they might dig for gold. He, in turn, asked miners in his saloon the places they would recommend. They nonchalantly pointed to the side of a hill above the settlement. The easterners dug, came back to the saloon with some rock for identification, and, as one account says, "The piece of rock was 'blossom' stuff, richer than anything yet discovered in the camp."[55] The mine and the town were rechristened "Greenhorn" as a result.

The camp of 2,000 people prospered and even supported a newspaper— the *Greenhorn News.*

A water system of wooden pipes which channeled fresh water to homes was built from Vinegar Hill.

The settlement straddled the Grant-Baker county line, with the post office established in the Baker County section in 1902.

One of the best-producing mines was the Greenhorn. It and others ultimately became non-productive, and the town was deserted.

The original claim cabin, jail, and several other weathered structures remain.

A building at Greenhorn propped up by logs. The 53.58 acres of private land at 6,500 feet make the settlement the smallest and highest incorporated town in Oregon.

Greenhorn — *Oregon Historical Society.*

Henryville was on the east bank of Isthmus Inlet, about eight miles from Coos Bay.

The town's hopes were based on coal. It has been written, "Somebody's money went into the ground—hundreds of dollars—tunnels, trestles, bunkers, docks, houses for the men and their families—money sunk."[56]

Steven Megeath was the first postmaster of the post office established in January 1875. A couple of years later the post office was discontinued.

Rotting parts of Henryville still remain along Highway 101 between Coos Bay and Coquille.

The Henryville coal mine — *Oregon Historical Society.*

Homestead, on the Snake River northeast of Baker, was a copper mining town on the eastern edge of what was known as "the copper belt."

Although it was known in the early 1890s that minerals existed in the area, it was not until the Iron Dyke mine was established in 1897 that the area began to boom.

At first, iron was discovered at the Iron Dyke, but copper was found below the iron deposits and in other locations.

Ore shipments waited until a railroad line was completed from Huntington to Homestead in 1909.

During World War I the town was the scene of extensive mining operations, but these ceased in 1922, and, as one observer put it, "since then its development has been limited by its inaccessibility, the hard basalt rock in which the deposits lie, and the present lack of railroad facilities."[66]

Mine dumps, houses, machinery, mine buildings, and remnants of a tram mark the spot of this mining camp.

Almost totally deserted Homestead is one of Oregon's most extensive ghost towns.

The mining settlement of **Horse Heaven** was founded one dozen or so miles east of Ashwood, in north central Oregon.

Cinnabar was probably found in the area in 1933 by two prospectors named Champion and Kenton. The discovery was located on the divide between Cherry and Muddy creeks. A few years later the Crystal Syndicate was operating the mines, called the Horse Heaven mines. In 1936 the Sun Oil Company bought the mines and operated them until 1944. It has been reported that 100,000 tons of ore were removed from the area.

A twenty-ton mill and reduction furnace produced 15,000 flasks of mercury valued at $7 million. The mill burned in 1946.

One estimate places the population of the settlement at "somewhat over a hundred," with several cabins, bunkhouses, a cook house, some office buildings, a schoolhouse with fifteen students, and "uncounted numbers of rattlesnakes."[57]

Scattered cabins, a loading tipple, a roasting furnace, mine dumps, and other ruins mark the spot of what *may* have been Horse Heaven—but what may also have been only buildings located near the mines.

Howard was situated northeast of Prineville on Highway 26.

Because the gold camp was located at the mouth of Scissors Creek, it was originally known as Scissorsville.

At one time the Almaden Gold and Quicksilver Company produced mercury there.[58]

Some structures and ruins of a gold mine remain.[59]

Jacksonville probably dates back to 1852, when pay dirt was discovered along Jackson Creek.[60] At one time the town may have been called "Jackson-creek Camp."[61]

During the first full winter of Jacksonville's existence, supplies could not be packed in from Scottsburg or Crescent City. Flour sold for $1.00 to $1.50 per pound; potatoes for 80 cents to $1.00 per pound. There was no salt in the settlement. However, it is recounted that "Apler and McKenney, a merchant, had a keg of very salty butter, too strong and old to eat. He rendered or melted

Mining in Jacksonville on C Street between 4th and 5th streets, 1940. This modern-day venture netted $40,000 in gold — *Southern Oregon Historical Society.*

the butter and the salt settled at the bottom; he sold [it] for three dollars per ounce to the miners who had no flour and had to eat poor deer meat (caught in the deep snow) without bread, pepper, or salt."[62]

The hotel at Jacksonville, which sold meals for $1.50 to $2.00, kept a "bouncer" at the dining room door to collect money in advance. Those who had no money were clubbed away from the door.[63] The hotel was probably the United States Hotel, where President Rutherford B. Hayes and General William T. Sherman were once guests.

As Jacksonville grew, it supported the first newspaper in southern Oregon—The *Table Rock Sentinel*—established November 24, 1855. During this growth period, the town was named the Jackson County seat. It held that honor from 1855 until 1927.

During its early years, Jacksonville was plagued with Indian problems. To retaliate for the killing of two whites, a posse killed the first Indians they saw after the killings— two young boys, who were summarily hanged.

The Rogue River Indian War of 1855 brought the cessation of mining operations; people were too busy fighting Indians or hiding from them. Later that same year the In-dians were placed on reservations, and the miners went back to their diggings.

By 1867 Jacksonville[64] had grown to a population of about 800 (later it peaked at about 1,200),[65] including a rather large Chinese population. The Chinese apparently came to the settlement in 1853 and left in 1880. The "Celestials" dug a labyrinth of tunnels under the town.

Several disasters struck the town. In 1868 a smallpox epidemic took the lives of forty people. In 1869 the cloudburst-swollen Daily and Jackson creeks flooded the business section. A fire destroyed part of the town in 1873. A second fire struck in 1874.

But the town refused to die and is today a pleasant village of more than 1,000. Several early-day structures remain, including the J. A. Brunner building, erected in 1855, the 1856-vintage I.O.O.F. hall, C. C. Beekman's bank, which shipped about $30 million of gold to San Francisco and Portland, the Wells Fargo & Company's express office, and an old brewery. The 1884 courthouse has been converted into a museum. There is much of the past, but some of the present, in Jacksonville, sometimes called Oregon's liveliest ghost town.

Jacksonville, late 1850s or early 1860s — *Southern Oregon Historical Society.*

The restructured ghost town of Kerbyville.

Kerbyville (or Kirbiville or Napoleon[67] as it has been variously called) was an early camp in the Grants Pass area.

The still-surviving town was named for James Kerby (or Kerbey), who took up a donation claim there in 1855.[68]

The town—probably established in 1850—prospered, and in 1858 the county seat was moved to Kerbyville from Waldo. Officials used the Masonic Hall as a courthouse and built a county jail with six-inch-thick doors, but in 1886 the county seat was moved to Grants Pass.

The population may have reached about 500.

A couple of interesting tales have been written about Kerbyville. At one time, it seems that someone in a neighboring mining town had ordered a pool table, which was to have been packed in by mules. The journey began at Crescent City, but the pool table never reached its destination. The mule that carried a key part of the table failed to show up when the expedition camped near Kerbyville. The mule was found the next day, dead. The packer figured that the gods were against him, so he established a pool hall in Kerbyville instead of going on to his destination.[69]

Another tale revolves around two feuding merchants. Their business establishments were on opposite ends of town, but whenever one man would come into the other's territory, he would be physically expelled. One day one man drew a line in the dirt and warned his rival not to cross it.

The challenged merchant answered by getting a knife and chasing his rival with it. They ran around a pool table (maybe the one the detoured packer brought to town), but the knife-wielder was not able to catch his prey. So he stopped short and held the knife blade in front of him, waiting for his enemy to come to him. The pursued merchant, unable to swerve aside in time, ran into the knife. As one writer of the tale puts it, "The next day the Kerbyville cemetery had a fresh grave."[70]

Gold, iron, quicksilver, cobalt, ilmenite (used in making paint), and infusorial earth (used in the manufacture of furnace linings) have all been mined in the area.

The Masonic Temple, several false-fronted structures, and a large oak "hanging tree" remain as reminders of Kerbyville's lively past.

The Kerbyville museum

Libby, originally known as New Port, was the location of the Flanagan and Mann coal mines.

The town was called Libby effective June 6, 1890, when Enoch Gore was appointed first postmaster.

Flanagan and Mann sold out about 1885, but the mines continued to operate on and off for almost half a century.

Today Libby is a suburb of Coos Bay.

Malheur[71] **City** was a gold camp that was spawned because miners from nearby Eldorado found placers and veins in the area—probably in 1863. But Malheur City may not have actually been formed until 1887.

The "Big Ditch" (see Eldorado section) served the miners at Malheur City for about five years.

One of the town oddities was the flower bed of Mary Collins-Richardson, proprietess of a store and saloon. It seems that her flower beds were bordered by half-buried empty whisky bottles.

Apparently many of the structures at Malheur City were nothing more than dugouts.[72]

In August 1957, fire leveled what remained of the town, and a few walls and a graveyard are all that remain.

Marysville used to exist near John Day. Today it is gone.[73]

During its heyday, when the miners desperately needed water for their placer operations, they obtained it through an eleven-mile-long ditch built from Indian Creek to their diggings. The job was done in 1864 with pick and shovel. As one oldtimer puts it, "Earning a living with a pick and shovel was no joke then."[74]

Milford was located northeast of Salem. The one-building camp was two miles north of Silverton, along Silver Creek.

Why it began is not known. How it ended, is.

In *Fifty Years in Oregon*, T. T. Geer writes of neighboring Silverton: "when my

A mule train near Mitchell — *Hazeltine photo, Oregon Historical Society.*

father moved there in 1855, however, it contained but one house, and that was on wheels, or log rollers, having just arrived from the town of Milford, two miles above, on Silver Creek—and when that house started away, it being a small mercantile establishment owned by Al Coolidge, Milford was entirely depopulated and has been ever since."[75]

The couple of hundred people who still call **Mitchell** home might object to their community's being called a ghost town, for in many respects it is not. The town, a trading center for a large mining and stockraising area, began as a stage station on the Dalles-Canyon City route. Although the town was begun in 1867, it did not have a post office until 1887.

One writer outlined well the disastrous events which beset the town: "Burned out, washed out, beset at times by desperadoes, Mitchell has had an unusually dramatic existence. In 1884 a nine-foot wave rushed over the bluff above town, filled the streets with boulders, some weighing a ton, carried away houses, wagons, and implements, and deposited mud and gravel on the floor of Chamberlain and Todd's saloon one foot deep. The town was attacked by fire March 25, 1896; ten buildings were burned.

"On July 11, 1904, a cloudburst precipitated a wall of water thirty feet high onto the town. Everything was destroyed save a few buildings high enough to be out of the water's reach. Only two lives were lost owing to the fact that the terrific din of the onrushing flood warned the people who escaped to the nearby hills. Two months later a smaller flood struck the town but as little was left to destroy the damage was slight."[76]

Certainly. with all that behind it, Mitchell deserves a niche in history, whether as a ghost or disaster-prone town; or perhaps as an Oregon counterpart to Tombstone, Arizona, a town "too tough to die."

Remains of one of four saw mills in the immediate Mitchell area.

Placer grew up in southwestern Oregon sometime before the turn of the century. At one time it may have been the largest settlement in Josephine County.[77]

The post office was closed in 1924 for lack of business.

The schoolhouse may have had up to a couple of dozen pupils. It still stands.

Not many other structures remain. Many were burned down, possibly by an arsonist.

Powers still exists.

David (or Daniel) Wagner located homesteads at Powers and returned to North Carolina to bring people to this new, free land. They settled in the area in 1873. When Wagner and his group returned, they found Chinese mining the region. The settlers frightened the Chinese from the land, probably in 1884.[78]

Later, Albert H. Powers bought the townsite from Wagner and in 1890 established a post office called Rural. In 1915 the town's name was changed to Powers.

Prairie City grew up more in spite of, than because of, mining. The camp east of John Day stood on rich placer deposits which the avaricious miners decided to dig out. It did not seem to make much difference that buildings rested atop the deposits. So the town was moved and the ground was mined. The citizens made certain that the new townsite was on the most barren soil they could find.

The town was granted a post office in 1870 but was not incorporated until February 18, 1891.

Prairie City supported a newspaper and became the terminus of the Sumpter Valley Railway from Baker. Later, hardrock mining was undertaken in the area.

Crumbling ruins of a cabin at Placer.

The former 1902 IOOF Hall at Prairie City; now the City Department Store.

Near Prairie City

Nearby was **Dixie Town**, site of rich placer ground. Perhaps 300 to 400 people mined in the area. The camp had two general stores, a livery stable, and two hotels, plus the usual mining camp businesses.

Quartzville was located in Linn County, northeast of Sweet Home.

The settlement was the scene of significant gold discoveries in the 1860s,[79] and again in the 1890s, but with the closing of the mines about 1902,[80] the town declined.

The settlement should not be confused with Quartzburg, in Grant County, site of the Comer Mining Company's cobalt mining operations.

Randolph came into being primarily because of beach gold mining. The settlement probably began in 1853.

The beach gold was so fine that some of it could be seen only through a microscope, but when the gold was detected and amalgamated with mercury, the returns were fairly good. The problems of finding the fine gold and the frustrations of separating the gold from the sand discouraged most miners, however.

A colorful account of life in Randolph was given in *A Century of Coos and Curry:*[81] "Storekeepers were weighing out flour, sugar, and coffee. Miners, up from the sluices on the beach, warmed chilled bones in improvised saloons, the steam from their sodden garments mingling with the reek of whiskey, wood smoke, and kerosene. Along the beach, honeycombed by the workings of the miners, at the mouth of the creek that is still called Whiskey Run, sprawled the town, a jumble of board and log houses with shake roofs, stone and mud chimneys, oiled-paper windows, and puncheon floors. Pack mules floundered deep in the mud of the streets . . ."

One report states that "Randolph-the-First" (there were others) was short-lived. "A terrific [sic] storm that lashed the coast in the spring of 1854 obliterated most of the gold-bearing black sands, burying sluice-boxes and shafts under dunes of prosaic gray grit. While miners loafed, waiting for the sea to sweep the worthless sand away, a prospector, later known as 'Coarse-Gold

Johnson,' made another find on a southern tributary of the Coquille. The stampede to the new diggings half emptied Randolph overnight.

"Randolph just faded away."[82]

But Randolph was not destined to die—just yet. On August 18, 1859, a post office was established at Randolph, with George Wasson as postmaster. The location of the Randolph post office (and technically Randolph) changed three more times before the office closed August 22, 1893.

A couple of hundred people still live in **Riverton,** south of Coos Bay.

Records indicate that at least 300 coal miners and their dependents lived there in 1898.[83]

The coal mined in the area was taken by steamer to San Francisco.

The settlement included a hotel, a couple of stores, seven saloons, a meat market, a church, and a sawmill.

The town was laid out by E. Weston during the autumn of 1889, with the first known settler being O. A. Kelly, a schoolteacher. He made part of his house into the Riverton post office, which was established in 1890. Kelly must have been a busy man, since he was also proprietor of the Riverton hotel.

Mines in the area have been spasmodic producers. The last one closed in 1940.

Sanger and the neighboring Sanger mine were both once named Hogum "as a commentary on the nature of [a typical method of acquiring] some of the earliest placer mines in the area."[84]

Before becoming Sanger, the settlement was known as Augusta, in honor of Augusta Parkwood, the first single person to live there. Soon the name was changed to Sanger, in honor of an early mine owner. In 1887 Sanger received its first post office.

The town has been the scene of several attempts at gold mining, but none have lasted long.

Scottsburg was settled by Levi Scott[85] in 1850 and became the county seat of Umpqua County before that county was absorbed by Douglas County.

The town did not grow much until 1852, when miners thronged to the north slopes of the Siskiyous mountains. Scottsburg became the metropolis of southern Oregon, with its prosperity based primarily on the town's function as the point of departure for the pack trains supplying the Umpqua and Rogue River valley mines.[86]

The town grew to have fifteen stores, a gristmill, and several gambling and drinking establishments.

A Chinese man with a fan — *Oregon Historical Society.*

The leading hotel was owned by a blind man from Kentucky, Daniel Lyon, a footloose guitar player and singer who made enough money in his musical performances to settle down and buy the hotel.

The *Umpqua Gazette* was published for a short time, but none of its issues appear to have survived.

The town[87] was washed away by a flood in 1861.

Silverton, east of Salem, is a settlement of about 3,000 persons. At one time, mines in the area produced silver, gold, copper, and arsenic.

It is not clear how **Sparta** got its name.[88] It appears that a man named Kooster found gold at the head of Maiden Gulch (near Baker) and that a camp dubbed Kooster grew up near there. But somehow, by 1870, Kooster had absorbed most of the nearby camp of Gem City or Gemtown, and the merged settlements were called Sparta.

Water was badly needed for mining, so the Sparta Ditch was scratched out from Eagle Creek to the mines. By 1871 the twenty-seven-mile-long, $90,000[89] ditch was completed, and the water that coursed through the ditch was used to mine several millions of dollars worth of gold from area placers. Apparently the ditch was built mostly by an estimated 500 Chinese,[90] although there may have been as many as 1,000 Orientals in the settlement at its peak, as well as 2,000 whites. Chinese also worked tailings left by their white counterparts. But they were continually harassed, robbed, and even murdered by whites who viewed them as competitors for the precious metals.

After most placer mines had been exhausted, many of the miners left, although a few took up hardrock mining with little success.

Sparta is still populated, but "thinly."

Sumpter was established west of Baker in 1862 and named by three people from North Carolina who called their log cabin "Fort Sumter." Later the spelling was changed to Sumpter.

As one observer put it, "For many years the camp existed by grace of the few white miners who explored the district and the hundreds of Chinese who followed them."[91] But a more solid city-building foundation appeared in 1896[92] with the coming of the railroad and the opening of mines in the Blue mountains. In fact, in the period 1896-1900 the population of Sumpter may have grown to 3,000.[93] It is estimated that about $16 million worth of ore came from area mines, which had twelve miles of tunnels in simultaneous operation.[94]

The miners and sheepmen did not get along—they never seemed to in the West. The miners' committee of vigilance reportedly told the sheepmen to keep out of the area on pain of being dealt with "until the Angels could pan lead out of their souls."[95]

A fire in 1916[96] destroyed most of the town.

The quiet village still exists amid the ruins of the days when the local paper asked, "Sumpter, golden Sumpter, what glorious future awaits thee?"

Equipment bound for a mine from Sumpter. Note wooden street — *Oregon Historical Society.*

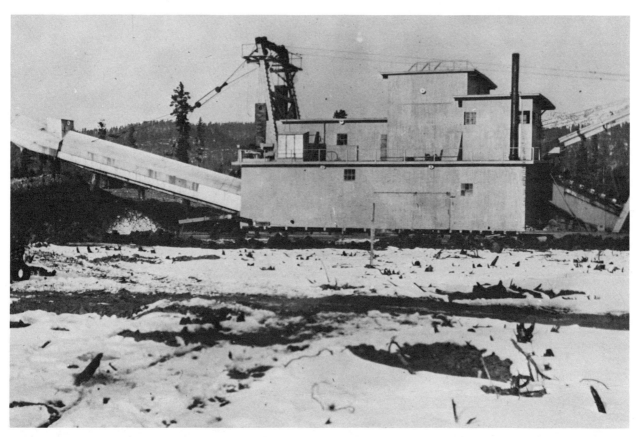

Powder River Dredge, near Sumpter — *Oregon Historical Society.*

The electric motor on this impressive dredge at Sumpter drove a drive belt 80 feet long to power the chain of buckets which gnawed at the rich gravels near the settlement.

Burned dredge ruins on the edge of Sumpter . . . one of three dredges to work gravels in the area.

The Sumpter town hall was once a store, with offices on the second floor.

This impressive building in Sumpter was originally used as a hospital and later became the home of the Masonic Lodge. It is now vacant.

The "Ichalaba" establishment in Sumpter. The word is taken from letters describing its offerings of IceCream HAmburgers LAundry and BAths.

Susanville was probably founded in 1862[97] by a group of miners who came to the area from Susanville, California.[98]

The town was strung along a single street, about one mile long. Remains of the town can still be found along the road that leads to the site.

The old stamp mill at Susanville is being reclaimed by nature as it quietly blends in with its surroundings.

Union Flat (Union) was a mining camp north of Baker when in 1862 the residents helped organize what was to become Baker County.

Little is known of the mining-era history of this small town of the Grande Ronde valley in eastern Oregon, but the town and the area were parts of the Oregon Trail saga.

The hamlet of **Unity** survives on Highway 26 east of John Day.

Although the area is now considered to be cattle country, the town was adjacent to the old Powder River mining region of the Blue mountains.

Utter City was a coal-spawned camp founded at the head of deep-water navigation on Isthmus Inlet near Coos Bay. Railroad tracks extended from the Carbondale mine to Utter City, from where coal was shipped to San Francisco.

The settlement was called Isthmus when its post office was established in December 1871. In February 1875 the name was changed to Utter City. The post office was closed in 1880.

Not only did the town lose its post office, it also lost the Utter City hotel. The building was put on two barges and floated down the bay to Empire to replace the Pioneer hotel, which had earlier burned to the ground.

The short-lived town left no trace.

Waldo was first called "Sailors' Diggings" or "Sailor Diggin's" because gold was found in the area by some sailors in 1851. There is disagreement as to whether the sailors jumped a ship anchored at Crescent City, California, and went to Waldo via the Illinois River, or whether they left a wrecked schooner on a beach and trekked across the Coast Range.

Waldo was one of several camps in an area that included Kerbyville, Althouse, Browntown, French Flat, Grass Flat, Allentown, and Jacksonville.[99] As mining excitement increased, it became apparent that mining codes were needed. During a miners' meeting in April 1852, those assembled at Sailors' Diggings decided:

1. That fifty linear yards shall constitute a claim on the bed of the creek extending to high water on each side.

2. That forty feet shall constitute a bank or bar claim on the face extending back to the hill or mountain.

3. That all claims not worked when workable, after five days to be forfeited or 'jumpable.'

4. That all disputes arising from mining claims shall be settled by arbitration, and the decision shall be final.[100]

The settlement ballooned into a gold camp that may have had a peak population of 2,500.[101] By 1856 Waldo had become the Josephine county seat.

Early mining activity consisted of placer operations. However, in the 1870s hydraulic mining was made possible by hand-dug ditches. The ditch serving Waldo was fifteen miles long and cost about $75,000.

For a time there were many Chinese in the area. One authority writes, "Many Chi-

nese were engaged in placering the creeks and were either ignored or mistreated by the white miners and merchants."[102]

But ultimately everyone left. The A. B. McIlwain store made of stuccoed concrete blocks, with iron doors and shutters, is the last remnant of Waldo, the site of what is generally considered to have been Oregon's first gold strike.

Whitney was not a full-fledged mining town, but at least part of its commerce evolved from mining. The settlement was situated on the narrow gauge Sumpter Valley Railroad line, which was used to haul lumber to the mining camps and carry gold from them.

A dozen or so structures remain.

Whitney

A mining camp originally called **Williamsburg** sprang up not far from Applegate in 1857 when gold was discovered along Williams Creek.

There may have been 1,000 miners living in the settlement during boom days. It was probably during the town's heyday that it was renamed **Williams**.

But the camp soon passed into oblivion.[103]

Because almost all old mining camps will inevitably slip into the same fate, please tread lightly if you trespass on any of these ghostly ashes of broken dreams.

Just as in the case of Washington, Oregon, too, was the home of many towns that were not thought of as mining camps. Nevertheless, their historical importance is not lessened by this fact. For the casual visitor, or for the die-hard "ghost-towner," these settlements sport as much intrigue as any mining camp that holds within its past a unique story.

The deserted Antelope Garage.

Antelope, in Morrow County, is about eight miles south of Shaniko. Various events crippled the town during its existence. When the railroad bypassed Antelope and was built to Shaniko in 1900, it looked like the end of the town. But the cattle industry kept it alive. Serious fires seared the town in 1898, leaving only one lonely original building that stands today. Another debilitating fire strick in 1964, but the tough town still clings to life.

Once-bustling **Apiary** survives near Highway 30. Some ugly scars of logging operations mar the terrain.

Aurora was a religious colony in Clackamus County.

Belle Passi is just below Woodburn in Marion County. Much of its past is reflected in a rather large cemetery on the edge of town.

Black Rock is a Polk County settlement on the Little Luckiamute River west of Falls City.

Boyd grew up and still exists in Wasco County of central Oregon. Several buildings, including a hotel, remain from palmier days, along with a mill.

Butteville is near Aurora in Marion County. At last report, a store was still in operation and a few houses remained. A historic cemetery is an attraction for some.

Champoeg, in Marion County, is a state park. No original buildings remain.

Chitwood is in Lincoln County of western Oregon. In addition to a few business buildings and homes, an interesting cemetery draws some modern-day visitors. A covered bridge is an attraction.

Dee is a Hood River County town in central Oregon. Robert Ripley's once-popular syndicated newspaper feature "Believe it or Not" once featured Dee as the only town in the world whose main street was a dead-end road.

Disston is in western Oregon. The Lane County camp was the scene of some gold mining at various times in the town's history.

Elk City is in Lincoln County, in western Oregon. A covered bridge is a main attraction of the village.

Marion County's **Fairfield** is gone. It was once a trade and transportation center featuring a riverboat landing. Today the old cemetery is the only vestige of this once flourishing town.

Flavel was at one time an Indian village called Konapee. The Clatsop County founders hoped the camp would rival Astoria to the east, but it did not succeed.

Fleetwood was founded by "honyockers" in Lake County about twenty miles north of Silver Lake in central Oregon. Nothing remains at the site but a signpost.

Flora is a scantily populated Wallowa County town. Ranchers and sheepherders still frequent the place, buy supplies, and now and then have a drink to toast better days.

Geneva is in Jefferson County, in central Oregon. Little could be unearthed about this town near Lake Chinook.

Grandview is a grand Oregon ghost town, about ten miles west of Culver, in Jefferson County. As its name implies, a grand view can be enjoyed from the town. Many views of an abandoned farming community remind the visitor of halcyon days before Grandview began to struggle down the avenue of dusty death.

Halfway is in extreme northeastern Oregon, just off Highway 86 east of Baker. Exactly what it is "halfway" between is not clear.

Hardman is a mouldering Morrow County town on State Highway 207. Stagecoaches used to stop here, but do so no more. The antique firefighting hand pumps that still remain could be used to fight a fire, but only three building stand, along with a quaint cemetery.

Homestead is in Baker County and on the Snake River about eighty miles northeast of Baker. Remnants of copper mining days remain.

Hoskins is a couple of dozen miles south of The Dalles in Benton County. The town is near the site of what used to be Fort Hoskins, a short-lived military post. The town is ghost-like, with a number of abandoned cabins dotting the site. The James Watson house, built in the 1850s, is said to have been the first plastered house in Oregon.

Joseph is a picturesque Wallowa County town. The grave of Chief Joseph is in the region.

Original **Kernville** is southeast of "New" Kernville in Lincoln County. A few old structures and hulks of boats remain.

Kings Valley is a Benton County town featuring several quaint old structures and a grist mill. A covered bridge is yet another attraction.

Klondike is a photogenic Sherman County settlement near Wasco in central Oregon. A number of buildings from earlier days remain.

Note the part-stone foundation on the building in
the right near Halfway.

A part board and batten–part siding structure at
Halfway is overpowered by a tree.

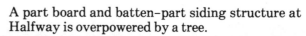

Lincoln is the site of an old riverboat landing. It is located in Polk County, in western Oregon.

Log Town is a Jackson County camp that has disappeared, except for its cemetery.

Lonerock is an attractive Gilliam County village. Several vintage buildings remain, including a diminutive jail.

Mabel, a sawmill town in Lane County, is now deserted.

Marmot supported a sawmill for a while. Now the Clakamas County town ten-uously clings to life.

Mayget grew up near Quincy in western Oregon's Columbia County.

New Era is southwest of Oregon City in Clackamas County. The most interesting remnant of days goneby is a grist mill. A campground and auditorium once used by spiritualists are also located there.

O'Brien is in southwestern Oregon along Highway 199. The town is on the eastern edge of the Siskiyou National Forest, in southern Josephine County.

A building in O'Brien now used as a boys' club house.

Olex is a Gilliam County town with some old buildings and an antique cemetery including markers of those killed by Indians.

Ortley is northwest of The Dalles in Wasco County. Many ruins remain in this short-lived orchard community named for the Ortley apple.

Paisley, in central Oregon's Lake County, is an extant cattle and sawmill town.

Pondosa, a Union County logging and sawmill town, features ruins of a large sawmill.

Richmond is north of Mitchell in Wheeler County. Several picturesque older buildings remain.

St. Louis was a Catholic mission settlement founded in Marion County in 1845.

St. Paul lives on, but the Catholic church is a reminder of pioneer days.

Shaniko, in Wasco County, was probably named for August Sherneckau, who ran the local stage station. One version of the town's naming relates that the local Indians corrupted Sherneckau's name to Shaniko.

Later the camp became a prosperous railroad, cattle, sheep, and wheat center.

Shaniko was the scene of conflict between cattlemen and sheepmen in the later part of the nineteenth century. It was one of the few places in the West where the sheepmen became the victors.

The picturesque Shaniko Hotel remains, as does the 1902 schoolhouse, city hall, and water tower. Wooden sidewalks can still be found in this, one of Oregon's most picturesque ghosts of its former self.

Shaniko.

The Shaniko Hotel.

The Shaniko school.

The Hotel Sky in Skyhomish.

A vestige of the past squats on the prairie near Tiger.

Shelburn was once considered to be the most rapidly growing railroad center in the nation. The Linn County town was also once an agricultural and sawmill and logging center. Deserted buildings abound in this western Oregon camp.

Sprague River is a Klamath County town. The settlement is near an old Indian cemetery.

Wendling was once a large logging town. Remains of wooden roads and logging camp structures abound in this Lane County ghost town.

Zena was born, grew up, and died in Polk County. All that remains of its life-to-death saga is a rock foundation pioneer church and a cemetery. Rest In Peace.

Notes

1. Muriel Sibell Wolle, in *The Bonanza Trail,* University of Indiana Press, Bloomington, 1966, p. 299 says the church was located near the "paterica" mine; but it was probably called the "Platerica" (see A. H. Koschmann and M. H. Bergendahl, *Principal Gold-Producing Districts of the United States,* Geological Survey Professional Paper 610, p. 299). There were other Spanish-sounding mines in the area, such as the "Llana de Oro."
2. Herman Francis Reinhart, *The Golden Frontier,* University of Texas Press, Austin, 1962, p. 57 says that it was named for Philip Althouse.
3. Wolle, p. 298.
4. Ralph Friedman, in *Oregon for the Curious,* the Caxton Printers, Caldwell, Idaho, 1974, p. 53, claims that the town was named for Lindsay Applegate. His brother was better-known, having served as one of 13 representatives in the first state election in 1845 (see Sidona V. Johnson, *A Short History of Oregon,* A. C. McClure & Company, Chicago, 1904, p. 244, as well as other sources).
5. Koschmann and Bergendahl, p. 226, quoting J. S. Diller, *Mineral Resources of Southwestern Oregon,* U.S. Geological Survey Bulletin 546.
6. Norman D. Weis, *Ghost Towns of the Northwest,* Caxton Printers, Caldwell, Idaho, 1971, p. 34, indicates the town was platted in 1899.
7. Lambert Florin, *Ghost Town Trails,* Superior Publishing Company, Seattle, 1963, p. 73.
8. Koschmann and Bergendahl, p. 216.
9. There were many Chinese in the area at the time. Rodman Wilson Paul, in *Mining Frontiers of the Far West,* Holt, Rinehart and Winston, New York, 1963, p. 149 says of the 3,965 miners in Oregon in 1870, 2,428 were Chinese.
10. Though not universally accepted, Wolle (p. 481) calls a miners' inch "the quantity of water that will escape from an aperture one inch square through a two-inch plank, with a steady flow of water standing six inches above the top of the escape aperture, the quantity so discharged amounting to 2,274 cubic feet in twenty-four hours." Another definition is that a miners' inch is the amount of water which can flow through a one-inch square hole, the hole being 6½ inches below the upstream water surface (Otis Young, *Western Mining,* University of Oklahoma Press, 1970, p. 122).
11. *Oregon,* Writers' Program, Works Project Administration, Binfords and Mort, Portland, 1940, p. 284 (hereafter referred to as *Oregon*).
12. *Oregon,* p. 284, says that one miner was killed. Wolle, p. 313, agrees. Charles Henry Carey, in *History of Oregon,* The Pioneer Historical Publishing Company, Chicago, 1922, p. 768 says two miners had been poisoned.
13. Carey, p. 768. John B. Horner, in *Oregon,* The J. K. Gill Company, Portland, 1919 and 1921, p. 169 indicates the execution was delayed three days following the trial "in order that opportunity might be given to correct [trial] errors, if any."
14. Giles French, *The Golden Land,* Oregon Historical Society, Portland, 1958, p. 31.
15. William H. McNeal, *History of Wasco County, Oregon,* n.p., n.d., p. 261. Another version of the naming of Bakeoven is that the baker lost his horse at that spot and stayed there for lack of transportation, according to French, p. 33. In *Oregon,* p. 390, it is stated that the baker "made bread which he sold to miners and prospectors on their way to the Baker [Mining] District."
16. Emil R. Peterson and Alfred Powers, *A Century of Coos and Curry,* Binfords and Mort, Portland, 1952, p. 111, quoting George Bennett.
17. *Ibid.,* p. 402. Between 35 and 40 men were employed as coal miners, but what percent were black is not indicated.
18. Peterson and Powers, p. 136.
19. *Oregon Ghost Towns,* Oregon Historical Society, revised edition, 1970, n.p.
20. This Bonanza is not to be confused with another settlement of the same name near Klamath Falls.
21. The post office was opened in May 1895 and closed in May 1927.
22. Stewart H. Holbrook, *Far Corner,* Macmillan, New York, 1952, p. 133.
23. *Oregon,* p. 285.
24. Friedman, p. 203.

25. There is confusion about this settlement. *Oregon* calls it Brownton. Reinhart refers to the settlement as Brownsville. However, that camp was "laid out" in Linn County in 1853, and later named for Hugh L. Brown, storekeeper and first settler there (for a more detailed history of Brownsville, see the *Dictionary of Oregon History,* Howard MacKinley Corning (ed.), Binfords and Mort, Portland, 1956, p. 37).
26. *Oregon,* p. 360.
27. Reinhart, p. 70. Wolle (p. 301) indicates "In 1858, when the camp was at its height, 500 men lived in or near it, and a smaller population occupied Hogtown, a sort of suburb."
28. McNeal, p. 198, indicates the post office was established in 1864 and that gold was first struck in 1859.
29. Some authorities feel Auburn, not Canyon City, was founded by men seeking the Blue Bucket discovery.
30. Herman Oliver, *Gold and Cattle Country,* Binfords and Mort, Portland, 1962, p. 20, says that in 1862, 5,000 miners were working the mouth of Canyon Creek to a point about three miles upcreek.
31. This may be so, for as Horace S. Lyman, in *History of Oregon,* The North Pacific Publishing Society, New York, MCMIII, Vol. 4, p. 188 writes, 1862 was the "biggest" year of mining at Canyon City.
32. Oliver, p. 24.
33. Oliver, p. 22.
34. Richard Dillon, *Humbugs and Heroes,* Doubleday, Garden City, New York, 1970, p. 252.
35. *Oregon,* p. 289.
36. Wolle, p. 321.
37. Lambert Florin, *Western Ghost Towns,* Superior Publishing Company, Seattle, 1961, p. 159.
38. McNeal, p. 259.
39. *Ibid.*
40. Perlite is volcanic glass or light-weight rock which has many small cracks that slightly resemble pearls. Treatment of the ores make them suitable for such uses as plaster, insulation, wallboard, and accoustical tile.
41. *Oregon,* p. 468.
42. Estimates of length vary. Oliver (p. 28) says it was 136 miles long, and adds it was dug by hand, mostly with Chinese labor.
43. Probably the West's longest system for carrying water was the 247-mile Eureka Canal in El Dorado County, California.
44. *Dictionary of Oregon History,* p. 99.
45. Weis, p. 18.
46. Horner, p. 145.
47. Prattsville was probably the first name for Gold Beach, in honor of F. H. Pratt, who organized the first pack trains between there and Crescent City. Gold Beach was also probably known at one time as Ellensburg, for the daughter of Capt. William Tichenor, the settlement founder.
48. Peterson and Powers, pp. 96-7.
49. Weis, p. 67.
50. *Ibid.*
51. Weis, p. 72.
52. Later Birdseye built a cabin from logs used in the stockade.
53. Portland cement manufacturing plants use this material. According to the publication *Oregon,* Oregon Commission of the Alaska-Yukon-Pacific Exposition, M. D. Wisdom, Compiler, n.d., p. 38, the company which produced lime from limestone at Gold Hill was named Carpenter and Allison.
54. Helen B. Rand, in *Gold, Jade and Elegance,* The Record-Courier, Printers, Baker, Oregon, 1974, p. 28, says the settlement was named for the rocky soil in the area.
55. Florin, *Western Ghost Towns,* p. 169.
56. Peterson and Powers, p. 137.
57. Weis, pp. 39-44.
58. Wisdom, p. 38.
59. There are differences of opinion as to the name of the mine; whether it was the Mayflower or the Ochoco.
60. Wolle, p. 304 reports that two young men discovered the deposits in December 1851, and showed them to two packers, James Cluggage and J. R. Poole, who, in turn, washed gold from Rich Gulch. Lyman states "Gold was discovered . . . near the present site of Jacksonville, on the place of Alonzo A. Skinner,

in 1852. Hubert H. Bancroft, in *History of Oregon*, Vol. II, The History Company, San Francisco, 1888, p. 186 writes, "In February 1852 one Sykes who worked on the place of A. A. Skinner found gold on Jackson Creek, about on the west line of the present town of Jacksonville, and soon after two packers, Cluggage and Pool, occupying themselves with prospecting while their animals were feeding, discovered Rich Gulch, half a mile north of Sykes' discovery."

61. Charles H. Shinn, in *Mining Camps: A Study in American Frontier Government*, Peter Smith, Gloucester, Mass., 1970, pp. 191-205 tells of an alcalde in "Jackson-creek Camp," which may have been Jacksonville.
62. Reinhart, p. 58.
63. *Ibid.*
64. The settlement was sometimes referred to as "J'ville," according to Ruby El Hult, in *Lost Mines and Treasures of the Pacific Northwest*, Binfords and Mort, Portland, 1957, p. 64.
65. Philip H. Parrish, in *Historic Oregon*, The Macmillan Company, New York, 1938, p. 178 writes of Jacksonville that 5000 people were there, "or possibly even 10,000."
66. Wolle, pp. 322-3.
67. *Oregon Ghost Towns*, n.p.
68. Some feel the town was established in 1855, but Reinhart mentions a pioneer physician and hotel owner—Dr. Davis S. Holton—as settling near Kerbyville in early 1853.
69. Florin, *Western Ghost Towns*, p. 149.
70. Wolle, p. 304.
71. Rev. H. K. Hines, *History of Oregon*, The Lewis Publishing Company, Chicago, 1893, p. 240, mentions that the French word "Malheur" means "unfortunate" or "unlucky;" as does Rand, p. 25.
72. As Lambert Florin points out in *Ghost Town Album*, Superior Publishing Company, Seattle, 1962, p. 149, it made sense to construct dugouts, since they were made of readily available material, and were relatively warm in winter and cool in summer.
73. If you take the time to search, ruins of what was probably the schoolhouse and other nonidentifiable rubble can be found.
74. Oliver, p. 24.
75. T. T. Geer, *Fifty Years in Oregon*, Neals Publishing Company, New York, 1912, p. 226.
76. *Oregon*, p. 448.
77. Weis, p. 60.
78. Peterson and Powers speculate that the date may have been 1887.
79. *Oregon Ghost Towns*, n.p.
80. Friedman, p. 127.
81. Peterson and Powers, p. 133.
82. *Ibid.*
83. Peterson and Powers, p. 123.
84. Florin, *Ghost Town Album*, p. 146.
85. Lyman (p. 188) indicates a Captain Lyman from San Francisco met Levi Scott and several other Oregonians and laid out the towns of Scottsburg, Elkton, and Winchester.
86. Bancroft, p. 183.
87. Most of what was inundated was the part of town known as "Lower Town."
88. Rand (p. 29) refers to the memories of pioneer W. H. Packwood, which indicate that Packwood, I. B. Bowen, Ed Cranston, and C. M. Foster each had a favorite name for the new settlement. They each placed their name choice on a "wooden top with four sides." The top was spun, and the side with Sparta on it fell on top. This had been Packwood's choice. That of Bowen had been Iberville, Cranston's and Foster's choices are not known.
89. *Ibid.*, p. 47.
90. The entrepreneur of the ditch project appears to have been W. H. Packwood, whose hand-written memoirs are quoted in *Gold, Jade and Elegance* by Helen B. Rand, p. 47. On the same page Rand quotes Packwood as saying of the Chinese in Sparta, "You could smell the opium a mile away."
91. *Oregon*, pp. 284-5.
92. *The Sunset Travel Guide to Oregon*, Lane Books, Menlo Park, California, 1968, p. 67, gives the date as 1895.
93. *Oregon*, p. 285.
94. *Ibid.*
95. *Ibid.*

96. *The Sunset Travel Guide to Oregon,* p. 67, gives the date as 1915.
97. *Oregon,* Friedman, p. 212.
98. Weis (p. 19) states it was once called "Upper Camp," and was established in 1864 as a gold camp, which received its present name in 1901 "when miners lifted the post office from the rival camp downstream." He also states quartz prospecting began in the area about 1869, supposedly after the settlement was founded, which would be a rather non-typical pattern.
99. Wisdom (p. 37) mentioned the Takilma copper smelter at Waldo, but TAKILMA appears to have been a town in its own right in the center of extensive copper mining activities. It was located about four miles from Waldo.
100. Oscar O. Winther, *The Great Northwest,* Alfred A. Knopf, New York, 1947, p. 221. Wolle (p. 298) also quotes this code, but in article one, stipulated that fifty "cubic" rather than "linear" yards constitute a creek bed claim.
101. *Oregon,* p. 362.
102. Wolle, p. 298.
103. *Oregon,* p. 327.

INDEX

Washington

Oregon

Ghost Towns of Washington and Oregon *was typeset in the Century Textbook Roman style by B. Vader Phototypesetting of Fort Collins, Colorado. Pruett Press/O'Hara Corporation of Boulder, Colorado, printed the book on a sixty pound Hopper Natural Bulkopaque paper stock, and Roswell Bookbinding of Phoenix, Arizona, furnished the case binding. The interior of* Ghost Towns of Washington and Oregon *was designed by Robert F. Wilson.*

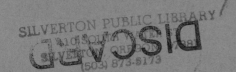
DATE DUE